NEW MEXICO
FIESTAS

A HISTORY OF MUSIC, DANCE & FANDANGO

Ray John de Aragón | Foreword by Matt Martínez

THE
History
PRESS

Published by The History Press
Charleston, SC
www.historypress.com

Front cover, top center: Folk dancers image courtesy of Frances Lujan; *bottom*: Los Abeytas image courtesy of Velma Salazar.
Back cover, bottom: Fabiola C. de Baca, photo courtesy of Albuquerque Parks and Recreation Department.

Unless otherwise noted, all images are from the author's collection.

First published 2023

Manufactured in the United States

ISBN 9781467154000

Library of Congress Control Number: 2023932164

Notice: The information in this book is true and complete to the best of our knowledge. It is offered without guarantee on the part of the author or The History Press. The author and The History Press disclaim all liability in connection with the use of this book.

The Spanish word *sobresaliente*, meaning "of the highest mark," "remarkable," "outstanding" and "distinguished," certainly refers to many of the Hispano/Latino sons and daughters of New Mexico. These prominent individuals and leaders in the state and country serve as role models for all Hispanic adults, youth and children. I was privileged and honored to have met, corresponded with and interacted with many of the individuals I am committing this work to.

These prominent individuals from New Mexico include Dr. Sabine Ulibarri, former head of the Department of Modern Foreign Languages at the University of New Mexico. Dr. Sabine was always proud of the fact that he came from the small village of Tierra Amarilla and became a member of the Real Academia Española (the Spanish Royal Academy) in Spain. Edward Romero from Albuquerque was nominated and appointed U.S. ambassador to Spain and was presented with an award by the king and queen. Fray Angélico Chávez from Santa Clara / Wagon Mound was an eminent writer, researcher and archivist. A statue honoring him is in Santa Fe, at the Fray Angélico Chávez Library located at the New Mexico History Museum.

Fabiola Cabeza de Baca, whom I interviewed along with others, was incomparable in setting the pace for Hispanic women everywhere in the United States, as was Concha Ortiz y Pino de Kleven. Antonia Apodaca, from my hometown of Las Vegas, always glowed with enthusiasm while playing and preserving New Mexico's Spanish folk music. Julia Sánchez, the wife of Dr. Willie Sánchez, vice-president of New Mexico Highlands University, showed the same zeal promoting and teaching New Mexico folk dance. Alberto "Al Hurricane" Sánchez, the "Godfather of New Mexico Music," inspired and always nurtured other Hispanic musicians and promoted New Mexico music.

Dr. Joseph Sánchez has been actively involved with the National Park Service and is the director of the Spanish Colonial Resource Center at UNM. Rudolfo Anaya, from Santa Rosa, is the author of the novel *Bless Me, Ultima*, which put New Mexico's Hispanic fiction on the national and world stages. A statue honoring him as a native son was erected in Santa Rosa. Ed Lujan is a founder and former president of the board of directors of the National Hispanic Cultural Center, and Dr. Mari-Luci Jaramillo, also from my hometown of Las Vegas, served as U.S. ambassador to Honduras.

I also want to mention Dr. Carlos Vásquez, former director of the History and Literary Department at the National Hispanic Cultural Center; Herman Martínez and his wife, Patricia, from Hilos Culturales (Cultural Threads), an organization preserving Hispanic musical and artistic traditions in New Mexico and southern Colorado; Dr. Joe Sando, Jemez Pueblo Native American historian and recognized Pueblo Indian researcher and scholar; Charles Aguilar, preserver of Matachine dance performance history from Bernalillo, New Mexico; Dr. Maurilio Vigil and Dr. Anselmo Arellano; Dr. Gabriel Meléndez, for his outstanding contributions, and his father, M. Santos Meléndez; Hermano Supremo, Supreme Brother of New Mexico's Penitente Brotherhood; renowned civil rights advocate Dr. Henry J. Casso and our progenitors Aurelio Espinoza, Juan B. Rael, Tibo Chávez and Gilberto Espinoza. They have all helped in building self-esteem and cultural pride among Hispanic students in New Mexico and all New Mexicans by instilling and preserving pride in Latino history emanating from New Mexico to the rest of the United States. It is an honor to dedicate this book to them.

CONTENTS

FOREWORD

As president of the board of directors of the National Hispanic Cultural Center in Albuquerque, I believe it is important to preserve and promote Hispanic/Latino fiesta, music and dance. I am the longest-serving member of the board. In New Mexico, fiestas are the heart and soul of the state. Culture and tradition are our heritage. This helps make our nation great. It makes us who we are, helps us to achieve and creates inroads in our careers for the benefit of everyone involved with festivities and celebrations. I also take great pride in serving as the president of the Sangre de Cristo Broadcasting Company Inc. I also serve as a lobbyist for the television and radio industry. I'm especially proud of the fact that my family and I have been actively involved with fiestas in Las Vegas for generations.

Fiestas in Las Vegas, New Mexico, are special. We have had a Fourth of July Fiesta for 134 years. My family has been involved with the fiestas and the Fiesta Parade for generations. A special treat most everyone participates in is street dancing. You can see people enjoying themselves immensely from their smiles as they buy delicious items at the food booths. As owner and producer of KNMX Radio, I make certain we broadcast for three to five days all live music and ceremonies from the event to listeners in several states besides New Mexico. KNMX received the Station of the Year Award from the New Mexico Broadcasters Association six times. I also own radio stations KNMM 1150 AM and Q102.1 FM, the Duke City's super hits of the '60s and '70s stations. When I served as mayor of the City of Las Vegas, I made it a priority to fund the fiestas and get support through the city's chamber of commerce, the Las Vegas City Museum, the Las Vegas Arts Association, New Mexico Highlands University, Luna Community College, the Armand Hammer United World College and neighboring cities. I solicited veterans' organizations for additional support. I have also striven to promote and preserve the homegrown song and music of New Mexico, as well as the state's musical artists, with the goal of allowing residents of the state and the nation to not only listen to but also appreciate this distinct Hispano/Latino musical genre. It needs to be honored and awarded.

I believe Ray John de Aragón's work is important for many reasons. It tells our story of celebration, joy and hope. It supports Nuevo Mexicano music and performing arts. It details New Mexico's fiesta history, traditions, culture and heritage for all to read, reflect on and appreciate. It graphically lays out colorful, fascinating and incredibly rich customs, explored in fine detail and liveliness and presented in a way that we all can enjoy. *New Mexico Fiestas: A History of Music, Dance and Fandango* points out all the good things in life that have taken the world by storm.

—Matt Martínez

ACKNOWLEDGEMENTS

When one writes a book, how can one express gratitude for all those who not only contributed but also influenced in one way or another what is written? If it had not been for my mother, María Cleofas Sánchez de Aragón, and her influence, none of this would have come about. She taught me to appreciate and be proud of everything in our Hispano history, including foods, music, arts and dance. Other progenitors in our history who blazed trails were Fabiola Cabeza de Baca, Aurora Lucero, Cleofas Jaramillo, Concha Ortiz y Pino and Jesusita Aragón. These women are mentioned because, in one way or another, they impacted my writing. My wife, Rosa María Calles, is not only proud of her heritage but has also vitally contributed with her love and devotion to her genealogy and history, which is reflected in my writing. Don Bernardo de Miera y Pacheco's granddaughter María Josefa Bartola Calves married Andrés Calles II. Miera y Pacheco is one of the most famous cartographers and santeros in New Mexico history. Rosa María Calles proudly carries on her direct ancestor's history and tradition. To all New Mexico women in the long history of our state, whether they are of Spanish lineage, Native American descent or that of other cultures, I acknowledge all of them with this book. I also acknowledge those who mutually seek happiness, joy and excitement through traditions and fiestas. ¡Que vivan las fiestas! Long live the fiestas in this very glorious Land of Enchantment!

Opposite: Around 1890 in Springer, New Mexico, girls and women paraded through town, all wearing white dresses. This depicts an unknown celebration.

Introduction

HISTORICAL SETTING

I t can be stated without doubt or contradiction that it is the grandmothers and mothers who lovingly pass on their history, heritage, traditions and beloved culture to their offspring. And so it was when Spanish women pioneers and their families arrived in New Mexico in 1598. These Spanish ancestors sang lullabies, danced and played games with their children. They and their husbands left their homelands behind to try to create a new life and seek better opportunities. These women sacrificed and endured pain and sorrow. They not only struggled but also persevered and pressed on. They washed clothes, cleaned, cooked and taught their children and still found time to celebrate and experience joy with festivities and fiestas. Often behind the scenes, Spanish women toiled and prepared everything needed for celebrations of faith, joy and happiness. Connecting with culture and tradition is an integral part of fiestas, as are dichos, proverbs and religious observances. The dauntless women pioneers of 1598 in Nuevo Mexico passed on a selfless legacy that is still vibrantly felt today and has endured and will live on forever. Fiesta stories are told through music, dance and fandango.

In September 1931, José Cúbeles from Santa Cruz de la Cañada wrote a wonderful piece about the Santa Fe Fiesta for *El Nuevo Mexicano* newspaper. The title, "Ecos de las Fiestas de Santa Fe," and the text express the sentiments of New Mexicans about the celebration of fiestas in the history of the state.

Han pasado ya más de dos semanas desde que las grandiosas Fiestas de Santa Fe se celebraron, y aun se desarrollan en la imaginación, como en cinto cinematográfica, todos los acontecimientos de aquellos días de luz y de color. Parece se perciben todavía música suaves y alegres que forman eco en los recuerdos de la conciencia musical; todavía se deslumbran los ojos con la sociedad de tanta luz de tanto color y de tanta hermosura, como bebieron en aquellos días; en lo alto de la sierra centellean aun millares de luces, que con resplandor rojizo y vacilante, alumbran la cruz sangrienta de los mártires; y en el corazón de la Catedral se elevan preces y canticos sagrados, que repercuten todavía en la Puerta, presidiendo a todo, está la Reina de la Fiesta, María Santisima; y por el aire aletean, como céfiro velador, los espíritus de los héroes de la Reconquista; y todo Santa Fe aparece todavía enroscado en los colores rojo y gualde de la banda Española.

La América toda, y de un modo especial el Nuevo Mexico, amaña España. Si España hubiera sido cruel con América, está la aborreciera, pero como que no ha recibido más que beneficios de ella, por esto lo ama y lo recuerda. Si los Estados Unidos no apreciaran la madre patria, no se hubieran celebrado aquellos ocho días de recuerdos españoles en San Antonio, Texas, la primavera pasada; ni los diez días Españoles en Los Ángeles, California, ni las Fiestas Septembrinas de Santa Fe.

Nunca se oye a persona alguna que hable mal de España, y se oye hablar contra el despotismo de Inglaterra, que, si bien que ha dado a los Estados su lenguaje, no le ha dado el cariño y amor de madre. América es acreedora a España por mil títulos, a cuál más importantes. Es un mito, una mentira, una calumnia que los Conquistadores recorrían América con el único afán de oro. ¿No sabe el pueblo que las carabelas, con las cuales Colon cruzo el mar y descubrió el nuevo mundo, fueron comprados a peso de oro y de perlas y a costa del Tesoro de la Reina Isabel?

¿Ignora acaso el pueblo, que el millonario Español Juan de Oñate desembolso millones de pesos, traídos de España, para los gastos de la colonización Nuevo Mexicana? Olvido el pueblo que todos misioneros católicos, recibían 350 pesos anuales de la Corona de España, ¿para gastarlos en beneficio de los indios? Y, lo que, es más, nadie ignora, que el mejor Tesoro que la madre patria ha dado al Nuevo Mexico, es su lenguaje, su religión, y la sangre de cientos hijos.

Es verdad que más tarde, ya América pujante y rica, España se llevó algunos lingotes de oro de los tesoros sobrante de Potosí, que España regalo al Papa de Roma, con las que decoro las Basílicas Romanas. Y para no desenterrar más de un hecho tiránico, la mayoría de estos oros fueron robados en alta mar por el corsario Ingles Drake. Los autores americanos admirados, dicen que los Conquistadores trataron a los naturales mayor que no les ha tratado ningún gobierno hasta prohibir a los indios que se dedicaran al pesado trabajo de las minas.

Los españoles trajeron a América toda clase de semillas, plantas, y árboles. Las primeras borregas que entraron en Estados Unidos las proporciono la Corona de España a la llegada de Coronado a Nuevo Mexico en 1540; después Oñate importo la oveja merina. Llego en aquel tiempo a estimarse en tanto la cría de las ovejas que el gobernador español Baca poseía dos millones de cabezas, y Chávez primer gobernador mexicano era dueño de un millón de borregas.

España intervino grandemente en la forma del gobierno de primitivo de América, siendo ella la que instituyo la primera Republica en los Estados Unidos, pues, bajo la presidencia del gobierno español, todos los años se elegio gobernador por votación, forma de gobierno que aun hoy en día perdura entre los indios, y la nación.

Over two weeks have passed since the celebration of the grand fiestas of Santa Fe, and the imagination unfolds like a motion picture on film of light and color with what took place. We can still hear the joyous music that still echoes in the recesses of our musical conscience: our eyes are still ablaze with the beautiful light and colors, as experienced on those days; on the heights of the hill thousands of lights glowed resplendent in red; they illuminated the bloody cross of the martyrs; and in the heart of the cathedral sacred canticles rose up that still reverberate in the heart of the community, and at the door, presiding over everything, is the queen of the fiesta [the revered ancient wooden image of La Conquistadora], *our Blessed Mother; and through the air fluttering like guardian zephyrs are the spirits of those heroes of the Reconquest; and all of Santa Fe is covered with the red and the gold of the Spanish flag.*

All of America, and especially New Mexico, loves Spain. If Spain had been cruel with America, she would have been abhorred, but since only benefits were received, that is why Spain is remembered and loved. If the United States did not appreciate this mother country, then the eight days of celebrations memorializing Spanish heritage would not have taken place in San Antonio, Texas, last spring, nor the ten Spanish days in Los Angeles, California, nor the September Fiestas of Santa Fe.

You never hear a single person speak wrongly about Spain, but you do hear about the despotism of England, that in goodness has given its language to the states, but not the care and love of a mother. America is accredited with a thousand titles [Spanish place-names and names of states], *which are more important. It is a myth, a lie, and a calumny that the Conquistadores traversed America with the desire for gold. Doesn't the nation know that the ships with which Columbus crossed the sea and discovered the New World were paid for with the gold, pearls, and the Royal treasures of Queen Isabella?*

Does the nation ignore that the Spanish millionaire Juan de Oñate disbursed millions brought from Spain to fund the colonization of New Mexico? Has the nation forgotten that Catholic missionaries received 350 pesos annually, from the Crown of Spain for the benefit of the Indians? And furthermore, no one ignores nor can ignore the fact that the best treasure that our mother country gave to New Mexico is the language, settlement, and the blood of hundreds of its children that has fertilized the sterile desert and the New World.

It is true that much later, America was rich and pungent, and Spain took some ingots of gold from the abundant treasures of Potosi that Spain gifted to the Pope in Rome, and with which the Roman basilicas were decorated. And not wanting to uncover more of the tyranny, much of these treasures were robbed on the high seas by the English pirate corsair Drake. Admired American authors say that the Conquistadores treated the Natives better than they have been treated by any other government, and that it was prohibited for Indians to serve in servitude in mines.

The Spanish brought to America many types of seeds, plants, and trees. The first sheep were introduced into the United States that were proportioned by the Spanish Crown with the arrival of Coronado in New Mexico in 1540; Oñate afterward imported Merino sheep. The breeding of sheep was so esteemed, that the Spanish Governor Baca [actually Mexican Republic governor Mariano Baca] *had a flock of two million, and the first Mexican governor Chávez* [Mexican Republic governor Francisco Xavier Chávez] *owned one million sheep.*

Spain enormously intervened in the form of government of primitive America, being the first to institute Republicanism in the states; under the presence of the Spanish government every year a governor was elected through votes, a form of government that still endures among the Indians and the nation.

Front-page notices in *El Nuevo Mexicano* of September 1931 declared that there would be a wide revival of Spanish colonial arts throughout the state.

Awards would be given, and exhibits for those works considered the best would be held. There would also be sales of original Spanish colonial works. All of this would be in conjunction with the Santa Fe fiestas. The notice announced the following:

The Society for the Revival of Spanish Colonial Arts that during the past years has been happily brought to fruition, and with popular interest, in the old arts of the Spanish Conquistadores has announced a competitive contest in traditional works that will be verified during the Historic Fiestas of Santa Fe.

As in other years, it has been contemplated that the ancient Spanish and those accustomed to works and the peculiar works have been fabricated from antiquity by the Spanish. During the Fiesta awards will be given to exhibitors by the committee they consider to be superior.

The competition is limited only to the descendants of Spanish Colonial families that reside in New Mexico. The articles need to be submitted in the name of the person that made them. No one can enter more than two articles in any class. Those that make similar articles like the artifacts cannot make any that appear of modern manufacture.

The awards will be given at the end of fiestas and if the owners wish for the pieces they presented to be sold, the committee will be in charge of the sales, as long as the exhibitor has marked the price asked on each piece. Those that wish to ship their pieces can send them to the Spanish Art Shop, Sena Plaza, Santa Fe, New Mexico.

Another notice from 1931, also in *El Nuevo Mexicano*, "Lucida Fiesta en Tierra Amarilla" ("Brilliant Fiesta in Tierra Amarilla"), reported on this event. The feast days of Santiago and Santana were being celebrated the ancient way on July 24–26. They would be celebrated with as much pomp and elaboration as in days gone by. The extensive schedule of entertainment included a grand dance in which a popular band from Denver, Colorado, Paul Nichols and the Night Hawks, would perform at the spacious hall. Fiesta patrons from the Española Valley as well as from Colorado were graciously invited to attend the many festivities, including local arts.

The same issue also promoted the Fiestas of Galisteo (July 24 and 25) on the Feast Day of Saint James. An outdoor performance of men on horseback with trappings would reenact the battle with the Comanches. The Indians were led by Chief Cuerno Verde and the Spanish soldiers by General Don Carlos Fernández. The notice read in Spanish:

He aquí el manifiesto al público: No perdáis la oportunidad de ver esta hermosa y varonil reproducción donde se dejarán ver las inmortales y sin igual hazañas de nuestros nobles e intrépidos Antepasados donde se dejará ver un rasgo de las formidables y poderosísimas armas españolas con acción en todo su primitivo esplendor.

Esto os dará un idea de las penosísimas fatigas y noble sangre que costo a nuestros intrépidos y bizarros antepasados hacer a la Madre España.... Esto a voz tocara el ala, refrescará vuestra memoria y dispertara en vuestros corazones un profundo amor.

Macario Leyba, the Tierra Amarilla Fiesta director, proclaimed,

Here is the manifest to the public: Do not lose the opportunity of seeing a beautiful and virile reproduction where you will see the immortal and unequaled deeds of our noble and intrepid forefathers where you will take notice of a feature of formidable and powerful Spanish arms in splendorous action.

This will give you an idea as to the grievous difficulties and the noble bloodshed and the cost to our intrepid and undaunting forefathers given for Mother Spain.... This Voice will touch our wings, refresh our memory, and awaken our hearts with profound love.

According to the newspaper, the Catholic nuns of San Juan were hosting a dance. Los Conquistadores, a popular band from Santa Fe, would be playing at the dance hall of Los Vigiles as a fundraiser to benefit the Church of San Juan. The sisters were raffling a new radio. New Mexico home economist and nutritionist Fabiola C. de Baca provided a recipe for a type of Spanish rice. Columbia Records offered albums of New Mexico songs and music at seventy-five cents each, including "Una Noche Serena y Obscura" ("A Serene and Dark Night"), "Los Diez Mandamientos" ("The Ten Commandments"), "Indita Mia" ("My Little Indian Girl"), "Amorcito Consentido" ("My Pampered Little Love"), "El Final de San Marcial, Nuevo Mexico" ("The End of San Marcial, New Mexico," a song about San Marcial, an old Spanish village flooded by the Rio Grande River), "Hijo Prodigo" ("Prodigal Son") and "La Primera Vez" ("The First Time").

Dr. Joseph Sánchez, author of *Coronado National Memorial: A History* and *Santa Fe: History of an Ancient City*, provides an appropriate chronology that corresponds with the essence of my book on fiestas and offers an introduction on Spanish colonial history. The eminent Dr. Sánchez served as the superintendent of Petroglyph National Monument from 2003 to

In this drawing by José Cisneros, the artist shows details of the entourage of Spanish settlers who colonized New Mexico in 1598. Cheering and celebrations followed drumrolls. *Courtesy of José Cisneros.*

2014. He has written several monographs for the National Park Service of the United States Department of the Interior. He received the Medalla del Mérito Civil ("Civil Medal of Merit") from Spanish King Juan Carlos l for promoting Spanish colonial heritage.

Once the settlers, who followed Governor Juan de Oñate to New Mexico, in 1598, had begun to settle into villages, their cultural values were evident throughout the places they established. Not only had they established a system of governance based on the Laws of the Indies, but they also practiced their religion, their music and the lore that had been transplanted from Spain. Having blazed the last portion of the Camino Real de Tierra Adentro (Royal Road of the Interior) from Santa Barbara to San Juan de los Caballeros, they had established a route that connected New Mexico with Mexico City. Indeed, the route was a transmitter of European traditions in terms of Spanish culture, language, religion, governance, laws, music, lore, and the cultural amenities, such as dichos (adages) and cuentos (stories and fables), that came with it. To be sure, the route was a combination of newly blazed routes that formed a corridor of both Spanish Colonial and Indian trails. In accordance with the Laws of the Indies, all first settlers, their sons and descendants who established new areas within the Spanish Empire, as done in New Mexico, would be honored with the title of Hidalgo.

Once established at San Juan de los Caballeros, the first capital of New Mexico, and later San Gabriel and Santa Fe, along with other villages, Hispanic settlers of New Mexico created a new world comprised of both an historical heritage as well as adding to the existing pueblo vertical cultural landscape with Spanish houses, churches, corrals, acequias, farms and ranches that tied to a new economy. Surrounding a given town, farmlands dotted the landscape with apple, peach, and apricot orchards as well as cultivated fields of melons, wheat, corn, chiles, and other assorted vegetables. Between the adjoining settlements were open ranges for pasturing herds of cattle, sheep, oxen, horses, and mules. In general, aside from stables or storage sheds for farm products, in corrals or within fences with small hutches near the homes of the settlers, one would have seen smaller numbers of domestic animals such as chickens, turkeys, milk cows, and goats, along with a few sheep and hogs for consumption. Farmlands with their attendant acequias (irrigation ditches) would have dotted the landscape along rivers. Outlying settlements would have been, according to the Laws of the Indies, located near such necessities as water, wood, and pasturage. Other food sources, as available in the wild, included fish, wild birds, and foraging mammals.

At the center of a given town, a plaza housed the institutions of church and state. Their structures formed a new cultural landscape to a given place. Each town had its cabildo (town hall) and its chief politicians: the alcalde mayor and his regidores (regents) of the cabildo. From time to time, as required, the governor of the province would visit the outlying towns. The business of the cabildo was to attend to the res publica, the affairs of the people. The cabildo voted on policies in conformity with the Laws of the Indies on all matters that affected the town, colony, or province. Beyond their social status, political leaders, the clergy, the laymen or the laity, itinerant traders, drovers, scribes, soldiers, settlers, and others in colonial societies seemingly had much in common as citizens of the empire that stretched from Spain to the Americas and the Philippines.

The ambiance of each Spanish settlement with its plaza, or town square and marketplace, during the colonial period was filled with the sounds of barking dogs, horses neighing, mules braying, along with those of cattle, goats, and sheep. At dawn, noon and evening, church bells made their clanging sounds announcing a moment of prayer and vespers. On a human scale, the voices of Spaniards, mestizos, mulatos, Indians, Asians, old and young, filled the streets and marketplaces within a given plaza. Their voices expressing laughter, conversation, or heated discussions would have been heard at once. On the outskirts of Spanish settlements, or not far from them, were Indian pueblos, which like their Spanish counterparts were farming communities, and rancherías (settlements of non-Pueblo tribes—in the case of New Mexico, Apache, Navajo, Ute, and Comanche communities), which lived off the land and trade. Such was the cultural landscape of people, animals, structures, and things between 1598 and 1846. Today, the world of the Latino and Hispanidad enjoy the rest of the story as reflected in fiestas, music, and dance along with Jotas Aragonesas, Raspas, and Fandangos throughout the world.

PART I

FIESTA HERITAGE

1

LOS MOROS Y CRISTIANOS
(MOORS AND CHRISTIANS)

¡Listos para ir de Fiesta! (Ready for Fiesta!)

Fiesta—the word itself brings out a feeling of exuberant joy and happiness. Las fiestas are a time to celebrate a special holiday or feast or any occasion that has been set aside for rejoicing and feasting. Sometimes, a fiesta involves competitive performances and exhibitions, but they always provide enjoyment for everyone involved. *Fiesta, música y baile y tiempo para gozarlo* is an old New Mexico folk saying meaning, "fiesta, music and dance and time to enjoy it." Since the first year that *los primero pobladores*, the first Spanish colonists, arrived in New Mexico in 1598, fiestas have been held continuously throughout New Mexico.

In community fiestas, men competed in skills of horsemanship involving the use of lariats and trick riding. It is a little-known fact that women also participated. Young girls were trained in horsemanship and often competed against men. Early Spanish fiestas involving *vaqueros* and *vaqueras* (cowboys and cowgirls) eventually evolved into the popular rodeos. Fandango dances capped off social gatherings. Bullfights were also held in New Mexico at one time. Dramatic presentations were a favorite with families. Spanish señoritas found an opportunity to wear their silk gowns and mantillas and use their beautiful and intricate lace fans. Traditional dances at events eventually included an array of fast two-steps, polkas and waltzes performed by couples through colorful street dances and dances on the plazas. A *bastonero*, or dance caller, called out popular dances such as the Varsoviana, el Vals del Paño,

Francisco Osuna (*left*) and Don Chávez (*right*) proudly pose in period clothing for Founders Day, a festival in Belen, New Mexico. *Courtesy of Don Chávez.*

la Raspa and the broom dance, in which the odd person out in a humorous musical-chairs dance had to dance with a broom. *Corridos* (ballads) were stories related to the sounds of musical beats and rhythms. These were sometimes somber when recalling lives and events of the past.

Dr. Sabine Ulibarri, a Spanish professor and writer and member of La Real Academia Española (the Spanish Royal Academy) and a New Mexico native, once stated with heartfelt sentiment:

¿Como sabrás algo del presente o tal vez del future si no sabes nada del pasado? ¡En Tierra Amarilla cuando celebraban sabían cómo celebrar! ¡Cada función tenía hondas, fuertes, y profundas raíces en la historia de Nuevo Mexico!

How can you know anything about the present or possibly the future if you know nothing of the past? In Tierra Amarilla when people celebrated, they knew how to celebrate! Each function had deep, strong, and profound roots in the history of New Mexico!

People have gathered to celebrate since time immemorial. Happiness and joy permeate the fun-filled air. Smiles, songs and laughter are not only seen and heard but are also contagious as the lightheartedness magically spreads. Worries and cares mysteriously disappear. People clap, cheer and even stomp their feet to keep up with the rhythm and the beat of the music. After many months of journeying across the Atlantic Ocean and across mountains, valleys, deserts and waterways, and surviving thirst, hunger, misery and death along the way, the early Spanish colonists of New Mexico were indeed ready to celebrate in 1598.

When translating, editing and recounting Don Gaspar Pérez de Villagra's epic poem *Historia de La Nueva Mexico (History of New Mexico)*, published in Spain in 1610, Dr. Miguel Encinias, former director of the Multicultural Enrichment Program at the University of Albuquerque and founder of the popular theater group La Companía de Teatro de Alburquerque and the light opera company La Zarzuela de Alburquerque, wrote, "Villagra's narrative poem, celebrating the heroic feats of the early Spanish settlers of New Mexico appeared during Españas Siglo de Oro, Spain's Golden Age. Events described in the literary forms of the period are tantamount to the founding of Jamestown, Virginia, in 1607. The actual settlement of New Mexico during the 16th to 18th centuries by Spanish families is little, or seldom understood."

The pattern of documentary evidence for the most part, apparently, rarely exists in the historical record, so the founding Spanish families of farmers and ranchers remain insufficiently recorded. The church/state history chronicling Franciscan priests in the mission fields and the administrations of government officials is well covered by scholars and researchers. For readers, the men and women who toiled in the fields or fought in the trenches while attempting to carve out a living are virtually ignored.

Both boys and girls rehearse to perform at the old town plaza park in Las Vegas, New Mexico, for the annual Catholic church fiesta celebration.

New Mexico has a rich multicultural heritage and history that demand further research, acknowledgement and recognition. This wonderful comingling of cultures requires more exploration. The first step in this regard is Villagra's monumental poem.

As the chronicler of the expedition and settlement of New Mexico, Villagra wrote that a fiesta was held when the capital at San Juan de los Caballeros was established. With words of praise, Villagra wrote,

> *Unas solemnes fiestas que turaron*
> *Una semana entera donde ubo*
> *luego de canas, toros y sortija*
> *Y una alegre comedia buen-compuesta,*
> *Regocijos de Moros y Cristianos…*

> *Some solemn fiestas that lasted*
> *For an entire week, in which there were*
> *Tilts with cane spears, bullfights, tilts at the ring,*
> *And a joyous comedy that was well composed,*
> *Joys of both Moors and Christians…*

In just a few words, Pérez de Villagrá graphically described events that would continue in New Mexico for centuries and, in some parts of New Mexico, to the present day. The horse riders tilted with iron-tipped spears fastened onto strong wooden shafts. These were also used in bullfights and with tilting at iron rings, in which riders demonstrated their prowess on horseback. This sixteenth-century author also states that a joyous comedy was composed and performed by some of the settlers, to the delight of all. Most important, the greatest pleasure came from the reenactment of outdoor theater, a century-old drama from medieval Spain called *Los Moros y Cristianos* (*The Moors and the Christians*). The festivities were the first European celebrations emanating from the Middle Ages in Spain to be performed in New Mexico in what would become a part of the United States.

Miguel Caro Mexican Dance Company dancer Margaret Perea poses in front of a massive effigy of San Felipe in Old Town Albuquerque before performing. *Courtesy of Margaret Perea.*

Muslim control of the Iberian Peninsula lasted from the eighth to the fifteenth century. For hundreds of years, there were strong pockets of resistance among the Spanish Christians against the Moors. This held off the total domination of the country by the Muslims. They considered the taking over of Europe a preordained order by Allah. The Moors were driven by a quest they called a jihad ("holy war"). What the Moors did not expect was that Spanish Christians believed it was their God-given right and solemn duty to protect their land and the rest of Europe. Countless battles took place, and many lives were lost. When the unification of Spain took place with the marriage of King Fernando de Aragón and Queen Isabella of Castilla, the Reconquista, or reconquest, of the peninsula occurred in 1492.

The Reconquista saw the birth of a vast celebration commemorating the victory, which was also celebrated in New Mexico in 1598 and for succeeding centuries throughout Spain and Spanish America. A white, wooden cross was placed in the center of an altar draped with a white cloth on an open plaza. Village actors dressed in costumes to represent either Moors or Christians

When the Spanish settlers entered New Mexico territory in 1598, they held feast days. A large celebration included an epic performance, *Moros y Cristianos* (*The Moors & Christians*).

held mock battles. Performers dressed in helmets used real or wood swords, lances, shields, colorful costumes and whatever paraphernalia was believed to represent the dress of the Moors. This historic folk drama begins with a Christian narrator shouting,

> *¡Alarma, noble español!*
> *Que los turcos se han robado*
> *La Santa Cruz y ya tienen*
> *El Castillo amurallado.*

> *Sound the alarm, oh noble Spaniard!*
> *The Turks have stolen*
> *Our Holy Cross and they have*
> *The castle fortified with walls.*

A Moorish leader interjects,

> *Cristiano, la prenda está ganada*
> *Cautiva la prenda rica*
> *Que entre los cristianos*
> *¡Es la prenda de más estima!*

> *Christian, the jewel has been won.*
> *The most precious jewel is captive,*
> *That is among the Christians*
> *The most esteemed jewel!*

A recently constructed adobe building represented a castle. Ironically, Spanish colonists followed ancient adobe building techniques that dated as far back as the early Egyptian civilization and that are found in ancient Middle Eastern countries. Following the mock battles, featuring clashes and shouts, those representing the Moors are eventually "defeated." The vanquished Moorish leader says,

> *Cristianos, ya su valor*
> *Vos tiene a sus pies postrado.*
> *Les pidáis por vuestra Santa Cruz*
> *Y por Dios venerado*
> *¡Que nos deis la Libertad!*

Christians, your valor
Has us bowing for mercy at your feet.
We beg for your Holy Cross
And for your venerated God,
That you give us our liberty!

The ageless Spanish fiesta Moros y Cristianos is an outdoor folk drama that is a cultural celebration of the reconquest and independence of Spain. It was and is celebrated throughout Spain and in former Spanish colonies. The popular event features parades, lavish costumes, music and gunpowder or fireworks. In New Mexico and many other areas, this spectacular event takes place during the feast day of Santiago (July 25). Saint James is the patron saint of Spain. It is interesting to note that early New Mexico *santeros* (folk art religious image makers) fashioned *bultos* (statues) representing Santiago riding on horseback and *retablos* (paintings on wood panels) of St. James helping lead the defeat of the Moors.

Although the Spanish colonists arriving in New Mexico were tired and weary from a long journey across the Atlantic Ocean and months of traveling via arduous trails and paths, they attempted to celebrate with some pomp and ceremony reminiscent of the festivals they left behind in provinces of Castilla, Aragón and León; the cities of Sevilla, Madrid, Cartagena and Córdova; and other areas of Spain and Europe. There were religious ceremonies led by the Franciscan friars. There was medieval music and song, loud booms from arquebuses and a fantastic meal shared by everyone. The settlers to New Mexico had taken along an extensive herd of cattle, sheep and swine. The livestock was supplemented with fish, duck and chicken. They also had plenty of grain, and there were wild vegetables. The music probably included *marchas* (marches) to the sounds of drums and *pasodobles*.

Villagra, in his 1598 epic poem, probably while taking notes on his journey for later compilation into his poem published twelve years later, mentioned a comedy that is believed to have been written by Captain of the Guard Marcos Farfán de los Godos. Historian Marc Simmons writes the following about Farfán:

On April 30th, 1598, the great colonizing expedition of Don Juan de Oñate reached the Banks of the Rio Grande....That same afternoon, the Spaniards held a celebration. Among other activities, they presented a play depicting the anticipated settlement of New Mexico. The author of the

Trail of the Painted Ponies master artist Rosa María Calles poses with the author and her prize-winning ceramic vase, Fandango. Calles often depicts fiestas.

impromptu drama was one of Oñate's officers, Capt. Marcos Farfán de los Godos....A canvas curtain stretched between two tree trunks to act as a backdrop. The bare ground served as a stage....Soldiers and friars took the leading roles....Capt. Farfán opened with an oration....Scenes depicted the hardships undergone by the colonists on the Trail....The pageantry of the day's events must have been impressive.

The events, which lasted a week, must have been striking indeed for the hundreds of colonizers and their families, priests and soldiers. The Franciscan friars packed everything they would need for the mission churches they were intending to establish. The missions were to be built throughout the territory. Heavy wooden carts with a long history dating to ancient Rome were pulled by oxen. The carts were piled high with belongings and formed a miles-long chain. Canvas tarps were pulled tight over the belongings on the creaking wagons. The friars journeyed with elaborate wood tabernacles, portable sanctuaries that served as containers to be placed on altars for the consecrated Eucharist during the Catholic Mass. The tabernacles, purchased from Spain and New Spain (Mexico and Peru), were hand-carved in the baroque style of the period and painted with handmade, water-based paints and were sometimes gilded. Chalices fashioned out of gold held the Eucharist (very thin unleavened wheat wafers for communion), pressed in ecclesiastical wafer irons. The wafer irons were embossed with the image of the crucified Christ and encircled with designs or words in Latin.

The colonial fiesta began with friars hurriedly erecting altars for Mass around the huge camp at dawn. The steadily rising sun and its rays captured a thousand campfires being tended. The pioneers stirred iron and copper pots, many placed on iron trivets. These were forged flatiron rings with three legs and feet and handles with rat-tail shaped finials. Trivets could be easily placed over flames for cooking on the trail. In Spain, these items were called *trepadas*. A wide assortment of other iron implements aided these late sixteenth-century settlers in farming and ranching, as well as for use in the home, including iron cutlery and lighting fixtures.

Spanish women accompanying colonizers took along an unusual assortment of items. Relatives and loved ones back in Spain provided them with material goods they felt would be needed in the new land. The settlers were in for a shocking realization that life was hard, but they made the best of it. Captain Conde de Herrera included in the Gordezuela inspection report of the period an inventory of what was carried in the trunks by his wife, Doña Francisca Galindo; their daughter, Margarita Conde; a sister-in-law, Doña Jerónima Galindo; and Anna Galindo. The items included the following:

Nine dresses, two of brown and green cloth, trimmed; another of velvet adorned with velvet belts and gold clasp; another of black satin with silk guimpe; another of black taffeta, trimmed; another of green coarse cloth with sashes embroidered in gold; another of crimson satin, embroidered in gold; another of red satin with sashes and gold trimming; another tawny color with white china embroidered skirt; two silk shawls with bead tassels, four pair of thin wool sleeves, one damask and velvet hoop skirt; four ruffs; four gold coiffures; twelve plain bonnets, six shirts; 3 pair fancy cuffs; one necklace of pearls and garnets with large, gold cross; a headdress of pearls with gold image of our Lady; some rings set with rubies; two pitchers; a small pot and salt cellar of silver; six small and large spoons; three pair new clogs; eight pairs of slippers; two pairs of high shoes; three pairs of stockings of wool and cotton; one bedspread of crimson taffeta, trimmed with lace; eight sheets; six pillow cases; three bolsters; two additional pillows embroidered in silk of various colors; two fine women's hats with gold ribbons; six pairs of gloves; and many other things suitable for adornment of women and the home.

The belongings carried by the female Spanish pioneers were indeed remarkable. Along with dresses, they also had silver perfume holders, containers for face powder and what today would be called lip gloss. They also packed silver mirrors and *peinetas*, which were intricately carved ornamental tortoiseshell combs, some measuring up to twelve inches. These were placed in the hair at the top of the head. Gold and silver filigree jewelry produced in Mexico filtered into the colony. It also came to be produced locally in New Mexico. Round chains of fine silver and gold-braided wires were fashioned into brooches, earrings and other adornments used for fiestas.

2

A FIESTA PROCLAMATION

On September 16, 1712, a torrential rain struck the Spanish capital city of San Francisco de Asis in New Mexico territory. Thunder and lightning rocked a vast area. In the surrounding hills and mountains covered with a thick forest of pine trees and vegetation, a few small fires began that were sparked by lightning. Dirt roads in and out of the city were inundated by the rain, and the land flooded. Homes and buildings were constructed with mud and straw adobes (mud bricks). The walls were also plastered with mud. Floors within these buildings were made of packed dirt, and the roofs were built with *vigas*—dressed, round timbers—and *latillas*—cut, dressed branches that crisscrossed the timbers. Over the roofs, straw was packed down, and the whole was covered with mud. The entire community, numbering a few hundred residents, was at the mercy of this unusual storm.

The Spanish government buildings, Las Casas Reales (the Royal Houses), which served as the governor's residence, office and officials' offices, known collectively as the Palace of the Governors, were inundated and flooded. Workers with various duties were also adversely affected by the storm. The Presidio (the military headquarters), located to the rear of the palace, provided some refuge due to two large *torreones*. These were towers, often built of stone and plastered with mud, with no windows, that could be entered only by ladder through the roof.

This area protected some people. Others had to seek refuge on higher ground, since the Santa Fe River overran its banks. This rapidly increased the flooding of agricultural fields and threatened livestock. Many residents

New Mexico Magazine has featured the Fiesta de Santa Fe on beautiful covers many times. The year 2000 issue celebrated its long history. *Courtesy* New Mexico Magazine.

had gone quickly to the massive St. Francis Church and its buildings and grounds. Men, women and children gathered within the church, praying for protection. No one had any memory of such an excessively severe storm hitting with such extreme force. Everyone was caught by surprise. However, what made this extraordinary day so much more memorable and significant was a proclamation made by the Spanish government officials of New Mexico that carried the weight of a royal decree.

General Juan Páez Hurtado, who served as the lieutenant governor of what was called the Kingdom of New Mexico, called an official meeting amid this serious storm at his quarters. He informed those present that he had been ordered to do so by the Marqués de la Nava Brecina. The order came some years before, and Hurtado was late in conforming to it. It turned out that the marqués was none other than Don Diego de Vargas Zapata Lujan Ponce de León, who had retaken New Mexico and the capital city in 1692 from a group of Pueblo Indian warriors. Many members of this group had also participated in an armed revolt against the Spanish in 1680. Many Spanish colonists, including male farmers and ranchers, their wives and their children, died, as did a couple dozen Franciscan priests. Some Indian Puebloans who supported the Spanish were also killed by the Indians who had turned against the government. A few hundred of the colonists and their Indian allies abandoned Santa Fe, traveled south to El Paso del Norte and remained there until 1692.

Don Diego de Vargas returned to claim the lost land of New Mexico for the Spanish Crown. Some descendants of the original Spanish colonists who had lost family members during the horrendous revolt returned, along with newly arrived settlers to El Paso and Pueblo Indians who had also fled during the "Exodus of Sorrow," which lasted twelve years. The 1680 reign of terror appeared to be over, as some Natives sent overtures of peace to the new governor. What had occurred during the departure of the Spanish military was the overrunning of the land by warring tribes of Indians. These included Apache, Comanches, Navajo and others who

Fiesta parade events statewide are often led by horseback riders in period costume carrying colonial Spanish flags in procession, as in this Española, New Mexico fiesta.

had a free hand in attacking the Pueblo Indians. Pueblo Indians were also fighting indiscriminately against one another. Governor de Vargas saw an opportunity to resettle and maintain the peace. He made a solemn promise and commitment to Mary, the mother of Christ, through a venerated ancient wooden image of her that had been taken to the capital city around 1635. This adored figure would lead them back to the city on a wooden litter. She was called La Conquistadora (the Conqueror of Souls). She was also known as Nuestra Señora de la Santa Fe (Our Lady of the Holy Faith). Don

Diego de Vargas promised that if they had a peaceful reentry, a fiesta in her honor and in honor of the Exaltation of the Holy Cross would be celebrated annually in commemoration of hope, peace, harmony and freedom in pursuit of happiness. Don Diego served as governor for two terms, including from 1703 to 1704. Juan Páez Hurtado served as an interim governor from 1704 until 1705, when he made the commitment to comply with de Vargas's wishes. Governor de Vargas died in 1704. His burial site is unknown, but it is more than likely in the interior of the original Saint Francis Church.

King Carlos II had bestowed the honor of Marqués de la Nava de Brecina on de Vargas in 1699. Marqués was an exemplary royal title of nobility that ranked below a duke and above a count or earl. It is interesting to note that the royal title of hidalgo, signifying a member of Spanish nobility, was also bestowed on the Spanish settlers of New Mexico in perpetuity for themselves and their descendants, also by the King of Spain. This is a reason why the land was referred to as El Reino de la Nuevo Mexico (the Kingdom of New Mexico). Other Spanish marquéses would serve as governors at the Palace of the Governors.

Lieutenant Governor Juan Páez Hurtado also served as captain general of Presidio officers and soldiers in Santa Fe. Faithfully obeying the orders of Governor de Vargas on that climactic day, he ordered all members of the *cabildo* (city council) to attend his solemn but enthusiastic meeting. According to the State Records Center and Archives of New Mexico (Series l, no. 179), those attending included Captain Don Félix Martínez, Regent Miguel de Dios Sandoval Martínez, Field Commander Lorenzo Madrid, council member Captain Antonio Montoya, council member Captain Juan García de la Riva and council member Francisco Lorenzo de Casados.

In honor of the Salutary Cross of the Redemption, Páez Hurtado stated at his home and quarters at the foot of Las Montañas de la Sangre de Cristo (the Blood of Christ Mountains) the stipulations that had been delivered by Don Diego de Vargas, most probably from his deathbed in the town of Bernalillo in 1704. These were to be addressed and written into a formal proclamation by those present. Hurtado went on to add, "The day of September fourteenth each year, this day is to be celebrated with Vespers [on the eve of] Mass, a Sermon [a homily commemorating the feast day in the Church], and a Procession through the Main Plaza."

Lieutenant Governor Páez Hurtado laid out several rules, including an oath to be administered by Fray Antonio Camargo, custos of the St. Francis Church, to all the members of the city council, Justice and Magistrate Alfonso Rael de Aguilar. The Regent Lord Marquez de la Penuela, governor

Los Bailadores de Oro (Dancers of Gold), trained and choreographed by Frances Lujan, is a senior-citizen group showcasing traditional dance. *Courtesy of Frances Lujan.*

and captain general of the Kingdom of New Mexico, served as president of the meeting. It was the duty and responsibility of the city council and of all succeeding councils from that day forward to collect funds for the fiesta, for the priest and the sermon and, most unusual, for all beeswax candles to be used. The proclamation mentioned that beeswax in the province was in short supply and very valuable.

Although the storm that slammed into New Mexico and Santa Fe left a widespread path of destruction, the colonists picked up the pieces and rebuilt. They had already experienced the pain and adversity of leaving members of their families behind in their beloved motherland of Spain. Those who came from other areas felt the same sorrow. After all, these intrepid pioneers had faced illness, disease, attacks and death during a long journey by sea and through rough terrain and desert. But they persevered and trudged on despite all obstacles to search for a new life and opportunity for themselves and their families. They found time to celebrate and to praise their holy image, La Conquistadora (Queen of Mercy, Hope and Love). They were happy to return to the land of New Mexico they now called home.

3

LA CONQUISTADORA
AND THRONE PARADES

t isn't by chance that the longest-running festival in the United States began in La Villa Real de la Santa Fe de San Francisco de Asis (the Royal City of the Holy Faith of Saint Francis of Assisi) in New Mexico. This was the capital city, founded in 1609–10, of the vast Provincia de la Nueva Mexico, the provincial major city of the internal areas of the Spanish Southwest.

An ancient Spanish wooden image of Mary, the mother of Christ, from an unknown date and brought to New Mexico around 1625 was lovingly protected and saved by the colonists. The carved image may date to earlier than the sixteenth century. The statue was said to have miraculously saved many colonists' lives. It was placed in the El Paso mission church with much care and reverence and was prayed to daily. In 1692, Governor Don Diego de Vargas also prayed reverently to this image and asked for Mary's intercession in reclaiming New Mexico peacefully, without loss of life, suffering or bloodshed. New Spanish settlers, those who survived the 1680 massacre and descendants followed Governor de Vargas, who traveled with those carrying Mary's throned image on a litter in procession in front of hundreds. This was called a *desfile del trono* (the procession of the throne) in Spanish culture, in reference to carrying revered images in a religious procession with prayers, singing and orations at stops.

La Conquistadora is noted as the "Empress of North America." This ancient wooden statue was brought to New Mexico around 1628. It is carried in a procession before Santa Fe's fiestas begin each year.

The massive Spanish procession of hundreds of families, livestock, provisions and belongings finally arrived near Santa Fe, and Governor de Vargas succeeded in retaking the city without much loss of life. Some skirmishes did take place, but these were inconsequential in the overall picture. Accompanying Pueblo Indians who had escaped with the Spanish returned to resettle their pueblos. In his promises to what was believed to be the miraculous image of Mary, Governor de Vargas vowed to proclaim the statue as La Conquistadora and that it be forever adored and revered as the spiritual symbol of Santa Fe and New Mexico. The governor also promised to erect a proper building to house the image and to begin and hold a continuous fiesta celebration in Mary's honor in perpetuity. He died before this could happen.

The annual event celebrated in Santa Fe and led by the miraculous image of La Conquistadora did take place in the eighteenth century and has continued to the present day. The venerated image is represented by a modern-day queen in the flesh who follows the image carried on a litter by an organized group, Los Caballeros de Vargas (the Noblemen of de Vargas), which begins and leads the fiestas. The event has been held from one generation to another in Mary's honor. Numerous early photographs attest to the fact that descendants of the early colonizers have dressed as Governor de Vargas, settlers and soldiers and have been joined by Pueblo Indians from various areas to celebrate Santa Fe fiestas.

Carmen Espinosa, who wrote *Shawls, Crinolines, Filigree*, a book about the history of Spanish dress through the centuries in New Mexico and other areas of New Spain, stated that there were many things held in common in Spanish settlements. For one, dresses, shawls, fans, *mantillas* (intricately woven headpieces), jewelry and tortoiseshell head combs, all items used by women, were passed down to the females in families in last wills and testaments. These were considered precious garments to be not only preserved but also taken care of and lovingly passed down for use on special occasions. Along with clothing brought in by trail that was traded for or purchased, there were garments produced locally by seamstresses. Not only patterns, but also different cloths were available. María del Carmen Gertrudis Espinosa prized the Santa Fe Fiesta dress she wore as queen in 1935 and posed for a photo with it for her marvelous book. For other women who reigned as queen of the Santa Fe Fiesta, it was an unforgettable experience.

Brittany Anna María Sandoval y Romero served as La Reina de la Fiesta de Santa Fe in 2016. The experience impressed her so much and left such an impact on her that she now serves as a dedicated member of the Santa Fe Fiesta Council. Brittany states:

> *Since I was a little girl, I dreamed of one day becoming a Fiesta Queen. For me, it all began when I was five years old and my grandparents Mary and Victor Romero took me to the early morning Novena Masses. A tradition I still practice today with my own children. I would see the young women walk into the church with their beautiful clothing and I knew that I wanted to do that someday. The women who served as La Reina before me were such great role models and their love for our traditions, culture, faith and our La Conquistadora is why I ran. It is why I am now a member of the Fiesta Council since my own reign. A promise made, and a promise kept.*

Santa Fe's Fiesta Queen is crowned by the archbishop of Santa Fe. Queen Brittany Maria bows before La Conquistadora, the ancient spiritual symbol and solemn pledge of fiesta. *Courtesy Brittany Peterson.*

The whole reason for fiestas is to honor our Most Blessed Mother as La Conquistadora. Being a Santa Fe Fiesta Queen is something that should not be taken lightly. It is a lot of work. You go throughout the community serving as a role model for other girls. You spread love and the light of peace. I still hold my time as La Reina close to my heart. It is one of the most precious moments in my life. Visiting the schools, nursing homes and communities and seeing people smile is an indescribable feeling. Walking in with a group of mariachis playing their musical instruments and singing fiesta songs and seeing many getting up and dancing to the beautiful music is truly magical! This is Fiesta!

During the early period of vying for the title of Fiesta Queen around the beginning of the twentieth century, certain prerequisites had to be met. These included being descended from the original 1598 Spanish colonists or those who arrived in 1692. Fluency in Spanish was also required. When Brittany ran for queen in 2016 and those before her, candidates had to be born in New Mexico, be of Spanish descent and be residents of Santa Fe County. They also had to be single and fluent in both Spanish and English and have a working knowledge of the history of Santa Fe and its fiesta history. They were also judged, according to Brittany, on appearance, poise, personality and sincerity. The Santa Fe Fiesta Queen winner is announced at the Gran Baile (Grand Ball).

The Fiesta Queen and several members of the Caballeros de Vargas, who carry the image of La Conquistadora on a litter from the Saint Francis Basilica, lead a procession. Brittany says this is a solemn and religious procession. Several miles are traveled to the Rosario Chapel, which was built around 1807. This chapel is located at the 1692–93 original site of Governor Don Diego de Vargas's encampment. The procession, which at times numbers in the several hundred, then progresses to the Palace of

The traditional queen's court includes Native American princesses signifying solidarity, friendship and peace. *Courtesy Brittany Peterson.*

Queens at the Fiesta de Santa Teresita in Albuquerque. St. Therese of the Infant Jesus Catholic Church and all Catholic churches in New Mexico host a grand fiesta on saints' feast days. *Courtesy of Reverend Vincent Paul Chávez.*

the Governors, then back to the basilica. The queen's entourage includes a diverse court of princesses. There are queens in many other New Mexico community and church fiestas.

Desfiles de los Tronos, the parading of religious images through the streets of Spain, is an ancient custom. Life-sized wooden images of Christ, Mary and the saints and other venerated objects are placed on small or large litters for transport. Hundreds and thousands of dedicated followers line the streets, praying to, praising and adoring the statues coming from churches, chapels and other holy buildings. This has been going on for centuries and is an integral part of Spanish heritage and tradition. The wooden conveyances can be so large that it can take up to fifty men to carry them. This is because the statues are surrounded by many other objects, including gifts of devotion, flowers, silver crowns, clothing and, perhaps, candles and other objects.

Streets in Spain can be very narrow. Some streets are so narrow that only one vehicle can pass through at a time. Many streets and roads date to the Roman era, when only carts and people had to pass through them. When stagecoaches came along, nothing changed. Streets could not be widened, as old buildings were constructed up to the streets. When the famous Corrida de Los Toros (Run of the Bulls) takes place, participants have little space in the narrow areas, which are crowded with enthusiastic onlookers. This obviously causes problems for all of those concerned.

Santeros in Spain produced wondrous and beautiful artistic works little appreciated in the art world. By using various woods, paints and sometimes gilding, these artists produced wooden sculptures comparable to marble and stone works of Michelangelo and those of ancient Greece and Rome. Carving wood is as difficult as carving stone. The fantastic works created by Spanish sculptors speak for themselves. During Holy Week processions in Spain, marvelous portrayals of the Passion of Christ abound. Various penitential groups, including women with roots dating back to the Middle Ages, also process. The tradition of throne parades and religious festivals arrived with the Spanish colonists of 1598, and this legacy continues into the present.

The origins of the colorful and fun fiestas that take place in New Mexico lie in the world-famous Fiesta de Santa Fe. This event is recognized as the oldest such celebration in the United States. It started as a religious celebration like those that took place in Spain as a tribute on the feast day of Corpus Christi (Latin for the "body of Christ") and included Vespers, a Mass at the St. Francis Church and the Marcha Procesional, a processional march. A group of designated Presidio soldiers, including officers, spent time praying at La Castrense, the military chapel. They then gathered at the church to carry the image of La Conquistadora on a processional throne. These throne bearers took special pride in being selected. These men considered it an honor and a privilege to lead the procession. The first processions retained a medieval aura inherited by the colonists from the early history of their motherland. The *paso* (float) bearing the image of Mary may have been adorned with flowers and other items, like those in Spain, which were much more glamorous. But the Santa Fe paso nonetheless received the same special care and attention to detail.

Devotees carried candles and accompanied the procession with graceful movements, all the while praying, chanting and singing. This was a poetic proclamation amid a warm and friendly environment. The earliest celebrations reflected vibrant and long-held traditions.

Don Pedro Ribera-Ortega always said,

> *La Fiesta de Santa Fe is nothing more than proclaiming, thank you to our Lord God and to our Blessed Mother for bringing us home from exile. To*

me the fiesta is comprised of two parts; a very religious thanksgiving which takes place in June consisting of novenas, and several processions, and then in September reading the decree written by Don Juan Páez Hurtado from 1712, proclaiming the purpose of our Fiesta de Santa Fe. The original ceremonies were inspired by also observing Corpus Christi. Descendants of Santa Fe's original Spanish families have been actively involved for many generations with our Catholic church, and our land of Nuevo Mexico to help with continuing our Spanish heritage for future generations.

Pedro Ribera-Ortega, born in 1931, was said to have been involved with the fiestas of Santa Fe as a young child, because his parents and family always took him to the events at the cathedral and park. He was honored by both the governor and the mayor with Excellence in the Arts awards for his historical writings on the Spanish history of New Mexico. He was also honored in Santa Fe as a New Mexico Living Treasure in May 2001. Don Pedro, as he was affectionally called, served as a member of the Santa Fe Fiesta Council and was its historical consultant. He was also editor of the Spanish-language page of the *Santa Fe New Mexican* newspaper. In 1956, Ribera-Ortega helped to found Los Caballeros of de Vargas, a group of male descendants of soldiers who accompanied Governor and General Don Diego de Vargas in 1692–93 on retaking the capital city of Santa Fe after the Pueblo Indian revolt of 1680. This group reenacts the Spanish reentry into what descendants of the original 1598 settlement consider their homeland. Don Pedro wrote about this as a return from an exodus in articles and multiple books.

Richard McCord, a close friend, said of the well-known researcher, "He represents much of what makes the city of the Holy Faith unique." Ribera-Ortega established and funded the Truchas-Ortega Research Center, located in the Spanish colonial village of Las Truchas. He purchased property and a building to help found a center for New Mexico scholars to do research and write about the Spanish history of the state. Here he placed some fifty thousand books, plus artifacts of New Mexico's Spanish history. Among the items are rare books from the seventeenth to eighteenth centuries he tracked down on his trips to Spain. McCord said that Don Pedro was "a most fervent champion of Spanish heritage." Ribera-Ortega's publications include the book *Cancionero Fiesta* and a booklet aimed at those who knew little about the history of Santa Fe and La Conquistadora. Ortega was the *hermano mayor* ("elder brother," a title given to a leading member) of La Cofradía de la Conquistadora (the Confraternity of La Conquistadora).

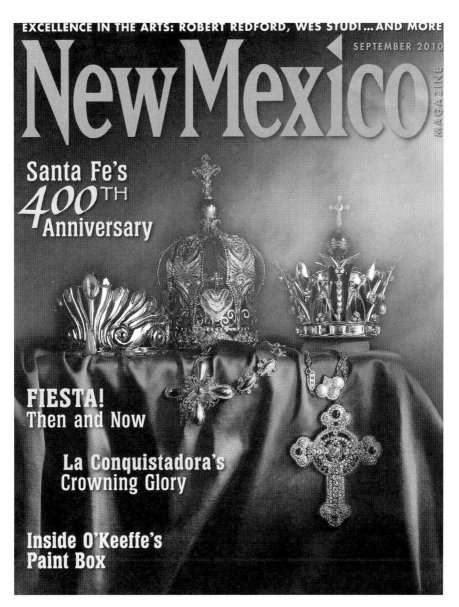

The September 2010 issue of *New Mexico Magazine* featured "Fit for a Queen, The Wardrobe of La Conquistadora," by Jaime Chevalier, and "Enduring Traditions: Santa Fe Fiesta Then and Now," detailing Santa Fe's 400th anniversary. *Courtesy* New Mexico Magazine.

Ed Lujan from Santa Fe vividly recalls the excitement of the fiestas in his hometown during his youth. He was actively involved with the creation of the National Hispanic Cultural Center in Albuquerque, New Mexico. He served as president of the center's board of directors after the facility, which showcases Latino heritage and culture, was opened. Former governor and congressman Bill Richardson said of Lujan: "Ed Lujan's dream of a thriving Hispanic Cultural Center in Albuquerque's South Valley has become a reality. Ed Lujan and the Center are synonymous." As the brother of former congressman and secretary of the interior Manuel Lujan, Ed Lujan tirelessly spent time promoting and pushing for the center and fostering the preservation of the Hispanic culture of New Mexico. With a great deal of interest and joy, Ed Lujan, who was born in August 1932, wrote:

Fiestas, including matanzas, and gatherings are very traditional in our Hispanic culture in New Mexico. We always gather for any important events such as baptisms, weddings, and religious events. I was born and raised in Santa Fe and our family went to many fiestas that were meant to give thanks to God for blessings that were given to someone or the community. The biggest one of all was the Santa Fe fiestas which generally fell on Labor Day weekend. It began with a solemn procession and then singing nine days before by taking the venerated statue of La Conquistadora from the Saint Francis Cathedral, now a Basilica, through the streets. This statue of Mary, Christ's mother is also called Nuestra Señora de la Paz, Our Lady of Peace, or Nuestra Señora de la Santa Fe, Our Lady of the Holy Faith, in reference to our city. The image was taken to a chapel where we all prayed a nine-day novena of devotion and thanksgiving. After the ninth day she was returned in another procession of joy back to the cathedral where a Mass was and is celebrated before fiestas could and can begin. Without this ancient Spanish ritual began by our forefathers and mothers, the Fiesta de Santa Fe cannot commence. This is the way it has been done from one generation to the next since the eighteenth century. My father was Manuel Lujan. He was the mayor of Santa Fe from 1942, until 1948. I remember my father saying he would always support the Santa Fe fiestas and the long history of the city. So, I and my brothers and sisters were always overjoyed to support the fiestas also. My brother, Manuel Lujan, Jr., and all of us were always involved with the fiestas of Santa Fe. All our family took part in fiestas as well as our friends and relatives. We were so proud when my brother was elected as a congressman, and, of course, Secretary of the Interior. All of us tried to do our part in promoting our rich Spanish history in New Mexico.

About a hundred years ago an artist by the name of Wil Shuster started another event by creating a paper mâché character out of old newspapers and chicken wire, I think, around ten feet tall or so, he called "Old Man Gloom." He tried to make it a figure that would attract attention, so they said he asked for help from other artists that were his friends or lived down the road from where he lived. It was meant for a gathering he and the others would have at his home. This figure has gone through a lot of changes. It became called a Zozobra which is a Spanish word for anxiety. Now it is meant to burn all our troubles away. Anyone can write his or her own problems on a piece of paper that is put inside the figure and then it is burned along with the problems. All cultures have their own traditions, and they are expressed in different ways. Learning about the different Hispanic cultures is an excellent way to not only preserve that heritage, but a way to begin to know and appreciate the heritage, and to respect one another's history.

It is interesting to note that Wil Shuster's figure of "Old Man Gloom," now called Zozobra, attracts a great deal of attention prior to fiestas in Santa Fe. But similar figures have attracted crowds in the Spanish-speaking world for centuries. An unusual throne parade traced back to the eighteenth century takes place in Valencia, Spain. This is called the Las Fallas Festival. It is difficult to translate *fallas* into English, but the closest meaning could be "without fail." This is most probably a reference to the fact that the festival always takes place. Giant structures are produced for this extremely popular festival, which takes place in honor of San José (Saint Joseph), the patron saint of the city. Local artists, sculptors, painters and artisans spend months creating massive images out of cardboard and other materials. The elaborate constructions of strange figures resembling humanoids and wrinkled or distorted figures with unusual appendages come in various sizes and can be up to five stories tall. They are burned on the evening of March 19 on the last night of a four-day celebration. Fireworks are strapped and lit during a Cabalgada de Lumbre (Fire Parade), to the excitement of the throngs of people who gather to view the massive fiery spectacle, with flames reaching far into the sky.

In 1860, a publication appeared in Spain from Valencia, *Fiesta de las Fallas*. This monograph by an unknown author detailed drawings, specifications and explicit details on how to create similar figures. It is unknown how many copies were printed, but the artists from Valencia, Spain, wanted to share the knowledge of their creations with the rest of Spain and the world so that everyone could make and burn such figures for a similar purpose. In

New Mexico, Wil Shuster and his artist friends made "Old Man Gloom." E. Dana Anderson, an editor with the Spanish-English *Santa Fe New Mexican* (also known as *El Nuevo Mexicano*), wrote a story about this most interesting and most unusual creation by Shuster and his friends. In actuality, the work was initially described as a framework six-foot figure of precut sticks filled with bundles of shredded paper gathered from around Santa Fe. This image was meant for a private gathering and party at Shuster's home.

The Fiesta de la Santa Fe (Fiesta of the Holy Faith) has evolved, grown and captured the imagination of the world, led by the now-ancient throne parade of La Conquistadora, the patroness of the City of Faith and of New Mexico.

4

FANDANGOS, JOTAS, RASPAS Y VARSOVIANAS

Anytime, anywhere people have gathered to celebrate since time immemorial, happiness and joy have filled the air. Smiles, songs, music and laughter are not only seen and heard but are also contagious. Lightheartedness magically spreads like wildfire. Worries and cares mysteriously disappear. People clap, cheer and stomp their feet to the rhythms and beats of the music and joyous dancing.

Well-known and distinguished writer Fabiola Cabeza de Baca recalled her early days in Trementina in the 1930s:

> We had a good time, people laughed and played. Everyone had so much fun at the fiestas. There was plenty to eat, with chile, beans, meats, and many desserts from old recipes that were so delicious. We had horse races, with both the boys and the girls. The girls often won. And when we danced, boy did we dance! We danced El Chotis, La Varsoviana, La Jota, La Raspa, and El Fandango. This dance from old New Mexico was everybody's favorite.

One of the earliest dances from eighteenth-century New Mexico is the fandango. This dance was widely known throughout the Spanish Southwest, including California, Texas and, possibly, Nevada. The dance also became popular in Spain. Fandango as danced in colonial New Mexico was a wonderful, slow and deliberate, and then a fast-paced, dance. This dance is classified as romantic and flirtatious, with obscure origins. It is known that

FANDANGO DANCE, 1790

Fandango 1790. Spanish colonial dances spread throughout New Mexico and became an integral part of all festivities and celebrations.

the dance was listed in a book published in 1735, the *Diccionario de la Autoridad* (*Dictionary of Authority*). It stated that the fandango was introduced onto the Spanish Peninsula from the West Indies. Regardless of its origins, the dance became extremely popular, and it was performed in New Mexico even in isolated villages and towns. It has been called the dance of the people due to the movements of the feet and the gestures of the arms and body. In Spain, in some areas, they dance El Fandango Antiguo (the old-fashioned fandango).

Each participant in fandango challenges the other with fast, pounding movements. The earliest recorded fandango melody can be found in *Libro de Diferentes Cifras de Guitarra* (*Book of Different Quantities of Guitar*), dating from 1705. This dance may have appeared in New Mexico between the mid- and late eighteenth century. It can only be conjectured as to where the dance first appeared in territorial New Mexico. Most probably, it was first danced at the capital city of Santa Fe. In many cases, this dance was accompanied by songs, such as the following stanza from Spain:

> *Era hondillo y sin soga*
> *Era poso donde caí,*
> *Y por más voces que daba*
> *Nadie me saco de allí.*

> *I fell into a hole,*
> *It was deep and without rope,*
> *And however loud I yelled,*
> *There was no one to pull me out.*

New Mexico fandango songs were like those written on the Iberian Peninsula. The following lyrics were written and signed by María Josefina in the valley of San Fernando de Taos and dated January 11, 1886. Lyrics were composed to be sung for dance and music. They displayed an inner sense of deep passion and longing. For example, "Una Mujer para un Hombre" ("A Woman for a Man"):

This carte de visite photo from about 1870 shows a Hispanic female kicking up her heels, ready to perform at festivities. She took time to pose for a photo.

Aunque Dios me hizo mujer,
Me dio noble corazón.
No tengáis a quien temer,
A donde hay satisfacción.

Yo te juro con desvió,
Y te llamo por mi fiel,
Que atada con un cordel,
Sera tu amor con el mío.

De cualquier otro me rio,
Yo no he hallado otro placer,
Es darte gusto hasta ver,
Quien de los dos aventaja,
Que este amor no se rebaja.

Aunque Dios me hizo mujer,
Si sabes que tuya soy,
Y que te estimo de veras,
Pésame como tú quieras.
Veras que con vida estoy,
Ni me presto ni me doy.

Digo que tuyo he de ser,
Solo Dios con su poder,
Me infundio esta pasión,
No tengáis en que temer,
A donde hay satisfacción.

Clara luna sin ménguate,
Lucero del bello oriente,
Si tu amor esta creciente,
El mio se halla constante,
Yo me he de salir triunfante
Con los que quieran vencer,
Que también es la mujer.

Halle posado el amor,
No tengas a quien temer,
A donde hay satisfacción.

Por ti mi prenda querida,
Hoy me vivo tan prendada,
Que me hayo determinada,
Arriesgar por ti la vida;
Mi voluntad protegida,
Tu semblante lo declara.

Pues solo el cielo divino,
Podrá apartar este amor,
Otro no lo apartara,
A donde hay satisfacción.

Aunque Dios me hizo mujer
Y de noble corazón,
Ausente de mi querer,
Sufre mi ardiente pasión.

De antes amaba constante,
Creyendo aun refulgente,
Y mi amor era creciente,
Pensaba salir triunfante.

En el altar de mi pecho,
Colocaba una pintura
con un nudo tan estrecho,
Yo me creía segura.

Cuando te estaba amando,
Dentro de mi corazón,
El crimen se fue formando,
Para ver separación.

Causa el mayor sufrimiento,
Mas no quisiera sufrir,
Porque tengo sentimiento,
Tan solamente por ti.

Fe, esperanza, y la latitad
Estas forman un vestido,
Y te digo de verdad,
De que tú la causa has sido,
Para vernos dividido.

Mas sin ninguna ocasión,
Por tu causa has sufrido,
Esta cruel separación.

Ponte luego reflejar,
Según es el pensamiento,
Es cosa muy singular,
Y ligero como el viento.

Hallándome yo capaz,
Y muy útil para ti,
Te pregunto ahora sí,
¿En qué pensamiento estas?

Mira adelante y no atrás,
Si algo tienes que sentir,
Bien no lo puedes decir,
¿O, en que pensamiento estas?

Although God made me a woman,
He gave me a noble heart.
You have no one to fear,
Where there is satisfaction.

I assure you without doubt,
You can call me faithful,
For your love and mine
Will always be together.

I would laugh at anyone else.
You will feel joy at seeing,
I have found no other pleasure,
Which of the two has the advantage
Of seeing that this love does not diminish.

Although God made me a woman,
You know I am yours,
I think highly of you,
Think of me as you wish,
You will see I am full of life.
I neither lend myself nor give myself.

I say that I must be yours
Only God with His power
He gave me this passion.
There is nothing to be afraid of
Where there is satisfaction.

Clear moon without waning,
Star of the beautiful East,
If your love is growing,
Mine is constant,
I must leave triumphant.
With those who want to win,
Which is also the woman.

I found love,
I have nothing to fear,
Where there is pleasure.

For you my beloved,
That I live so attached to,
I find myself determined.
To risk for you my life
My will is protected,
Your appearance makes it clear.

And yet only the divine heaven
Can separate our love,
No one else can divide it,
Where there is pleasure.

Although God made me a woman
And of noble heart,
Absence of my love,
My ardent passion suffers.

In the past I constantly loved,
Thinking of my love ablaze
And with my love ever increasing,
I thought I would be triumphant.

At the core of my heart
I hung a painting,
With a tight knot
Which made me feel secure.

When I was loving you,
Deep within my heart,
A misdeed began to form,
Of our coming apart.

Faith, hope, and with distance
You are forming an impression,
And I'm telling you the truth,
You are the cause of it happening,
That is pulling us apart.

More than anything else,
Due to yourself you've suffered,
This cruel separation.

Reflect on what you have done,
As opinions are set,
It is a unique thing,
And fleeting as light in the wind.

Finding myself capable,
And very useful for you,
I'm asking you now.
What are you thinking?

Look forward and not in the past,
If there is something that you feel,
Or you can't say it any better
So, what are you thinking?

José María Martínez wrote deep-felt words to the love of his life on July 27, 1863. He was likely a New Mexico volunteer during the Civil War and was stationed somewhere on the battlefield. Two major battles were fought against the Confederates in New Mexico, one at Valverde and the other at Glorieta. Martínez meant his sentiments to be set to music and sung. He most probably sent his composition to Eliza (Eli) by mail.

Eli

Deseo ver y deseo ver a Eli.
Yo deseo ver, y deseo ver a Eli.
Mi corazón me avisa a Eli he de querer.
Eli es mi esperanza, mi recreo, y mi confianza.
Deseo ver y deseo ver a Eli.

Eli es mi esmero,
Hablo con todo amor,
Oye mi querida Eli,
Mi corazón me avisa,
Que tu haz de ser mi esperanza,
Tus ojos son las estrellas,
Que lucen y brillan amor.

Es mi voluntad crecida,
Eli, mi prenda querida,
Deseo ser tu amante,
Con amor constante,
Eres mi razón de vivir.

Deseo ver y deseo ver a Eli,
Yo deseo ver, y deseo ver a Eli.

Eres mi amor y vida,
La cándida rubí,
Entre las flores escogidas,
Aquí están mis delicias.

En una ceremonia clara y fina,
Eliza me diste tu amor.
Las caricias, y tu pasión.
Con mucho candor.

Tu rostro soberano
Manda mi corazón.

Me das tu mano
Con mucha ternura,
Cautivas mi desventura,
Con resueño y amor.

Eliza, bella criatura,
Mi adoración,
Y ternura,
Se alegra mi corazón.

Deseo ver y deseo ver a Eli,
Yo deseo ver y deseo ver a Eli.

Eli

I desire to see and I desire to see Eli
My heart tells me it is Eli I should care for.
Eli is my hope, my pleasure, and my confidence.
I desire to see and desire to see Eli.

Eli is whom I care for,
I speak with all my love,
Hear me my beloved Eli,
My heart tells me

You are my hope,
Your eyes are the stars,
The shining light of love.

You are the growing strength within me,
Eli, my jewel of love,
I desire to be your lover,
My love for you is always present,
You're my reason for living.

I desire to see Eli,
I desire to see, and desire to see Eli.

You're my love and my life,
The ruby of my commitment,
Among chosen flowers,
Here is where my delightfulness lies.

In the ultimate ceremony,
Eliza, you gave me your love,
Your caresses and your passion,
With so much sincerity.

Your precious face
Controls my heart.

You give me your hand
With so much tenderness,
You capture my misfortune,
With vibrant love.

Eliza, beautiful woman,
My adoration,
And tenderness,
Fills my heart with joy.

I desire to see and desire to see Eli,
I desire to see and desire to see Eli.

One aspect of Spanish culture that has largely gone unrecognized has to do with poetry and song dedicated to horses and livestock. During the fiestas of old, troubadours sang to their beloved horses. Cervantes's Don Quixote cares about his horse, Rocinante, and his trusty squire, Sancho Panza, loves his mule. In New Mexico, Spanish cowboys sang to their horses. When Americans entered New Mexico territory, they grasped Spanish cowboy trappings and lingo and adopted Spanish Western song. In fact, some Western singers still sing very old compositions in both Spanish and English. Songs of the range are being continuously recorded and sung at festivals. The following ode sung by a bull is especially unique in that it displays a rarely written-about aspect of bulls and bullfighting in New Mexico history and tradition. This New Mexico bull speaks in the first person.

El Toro
Yo soy aquel toro bravo,
Que sacaste a fuerzas.

Si me vuelves a torear,
Te he de cornear de veras.

Soy aquel toro Amarillo,
Puntal tan áspero, y fiero.

Que tratas tú de ternero,
Aunque he sido bueno y novillo.

Dices que soy becerrillo,
De esos que no hacen estrago.

Si no temes a mi amago,
Mi respeto debe ser.

Yo enojado te diré,
Yo soy aquel Toro bravo.

Dices que soy Toro mocho,
De estos que aguantan el yugo.

Puntal me veo sacando,
Las encentras de un mal hecho.

Traigo dos reales del ocho,
En tambor de mis banderas.

Hablaras donde quisieras,
Para divertirme tantito.

Atorrar al becerrito,
Que sacaste abarreras.
Todavía piso las flores,
Que han mejorado en el monte.

Bramo de Toro chin chonte,
Como dos mil primores;
Y las terneras mejores.

Si me vienen agregar,
Y como Toro puntal,
Te advierto con regocijo,
Que te rompo el entresijo,
Si me vuelves atorrar.

Ya se va llegando el France,
Que me veo enojado,
Y si me hace otro lance,
Te paso hasta el otro lado.

Ya traigo el pelo arriesgado,
Y mis hasta muy de veras,
Para seguir vuestro lance,
Y para que yo descanse
Te he de cornear deveras.

Se inclinan a tus banderas.

The Bull
I am that brave bull,
That you pulled out by force.

If you fight me once again,
I will truly pierce you.

I am that yellow bull,
Rough, tough, and fierce.

That you treat like a calf,
Although I've been a good steer.

You say I'm a yearling calf,
Like those that do not make havoc.

If you don't fear my threat,
You should give me respect.

I angrily tell you,
I am that brave bull.

You say I'm a dumb bull,
Of those who bear the yoke.

I see myself piercing,
Those that have done me wrong.

I have two reales out of eight,
On the drum of my flags.

Say whatever you want,
So that I can have a little fun.
You wish to tie up the calf,
You have created barriers.
I will still step on the flowers,
They grow much better in the mountain.

The bull roared chin chonte,
With two thousand times perfection
than the best calves.

If you all come to attack me,
Know I'm a bull with horns,
I warn you with delight,
I will rip you with joy,

If you try to fight me.
The time is coming up,
I am getting angrier,
And if you lance me again.
I will run you through.

My hair is standing on end,
And my hoofs are too,
To follow your lance,
It will give me rest
And I will stick my horns into you.

They move down to your flags.

Fandango has experienced an evolution through the centuries. On the colonial frontier of New Mexico, most probably in Santa Fe, guitar and violin players provided fast and exciting rhythms for dancers, while onlookers clapped loudly and encouraged the dancers to go faster. Cheering and laughter filled the air. This was a genuine folkloric dance that accompanied other dances in time at community festivities and celebrations. Contrary to what has been written in the past, books were readily available in New Mexico for the local populace, since a majority knew how to read and write. One book that may have been available in New Mexico was published in Madrid, Spain, in 1764. A curious illustration depicts a couple dressed in the style of the day.

The brief manual covered Spanish dance styles of *seguidillas* (steps to follow with the fandango) and others that were similar. It stated that these steps could also serve with other European forms, such as Italian, French and English dance, by following the music. With the passing of time, terms such as *fandango antiguo* (ancient fandango) and *fandangoised minuet* were used, because fandango steps were incorporated in other dances. It is written that fandango was introduced into many stage and instrumental works of French and Italian composers. This well-known Spanish dance, still performed in some areas of New Mexico, spread to other European countries. It is now a main folk dance of those nations, including Portugal.

Dress styles for dance reflect what was worn in those areas during the periods from the eighteenth to the nineteenth centuries. For example, feminine styles in New Mexico for fiestas were fascinating, since these included inherited colonial clothing. Women wore *mantillas*, intricately

Las Fiestas featured fandango dances at Spanish colonial events throughout New Mexico Territory and were prevalent in other Spanish territories.

Los Tapatíos dance group directed and taught by Frances Lujan. Boys and girls excel when dancing, singing and entertaining. *Courtesy Frances Lujan.*

woven head coverings that could be draped over the shoulders. On the head, *mantillas* were held up by *peinetas*, tortoiseshell head combs that were carved in detail, some measuring twelve inches or more.

Another popular dance in New Mexico performed at events was the *jota*. La Jota Aragonesa, from Aragón, Spain, in the eighteenth century, was an expression of culture with complex dance steps and singing. This dance was included in *zarzuelas*, which were contests that took place at festivals. Guitars and drums were used. Themes for the dance included religion, patriotism and sexual exploits. The dance was used at all social gatherings, including parties, baptisms and weddings. It was a simple kicking dance with sidesteps that could incorporate many movements. Couples danced to loud, encouraging clapping. La Varsoviana (The Girl from Warsaw) was another dance performed during early New Mexico fiestas. Like most dances, its origins are obscure. It is known that the dance first appeared in 1850.

5

MATACHINE DANCERS AND ANCIENT RITUALS

Dr. Joe S. Sando, an esteemed elder and popular writer from Jemez Pueblo born in 1923, emphasized more than once that the Pueblo Indians and Spanish had a close relationship. Some do not believe this, because Po'pay, the well-known leader of the Pueblo Indian revolt of 1680, who was supposed to have come from the ancient Indian pueblo of San Juan, and his close followers consistently clashed with Spanish officials. Historically, there are few known facts about the Indian Po'pay, who is generally believed to have led the rebellion against the Spanish colonization of New Mexico. In fact, Sando wrote two relevant books, *Po'pay* and *Nee Hamish, A History of Jemez Pueblo, and Pueblo Nations: Eight Centuries of Pueblo Indian History*. Sando was born into the Sun Clan at Jemez. He served in World War II, attended Vanderbilt University and taught ethnohistory at the Institute of American Indian Arts in Santa Fe. Dr. Sando was former director of the Institute of Pueblo Study and Research at the Indian Pueblo Cultural Center in Albuquerque. At one time, he taught Pueblo Indian history at the United States International University. He received the Excellence in Humanities Award from the New Mexico Endowment for the Humanities.

I was honored to have attended several functions where I got to sit next to Dr. Sando, and we had in-depth conversations. He was proud that he could speak Towa, his native language, as well as Spanish and English. He said many Pueblo Indians are trilingual, speaking their native tongue and English and Spanish. "Not only that," he added. "They can also read in English and Spanish, making them unique among Native Americans in this country. I

Matachine Dancer, acrylic on canvas and painted frame, by Rosa María Calles. The artist researched and portrayed a Spanish colonial period dancer.

can read in Spanish." Dr. Sando was not only personable but also proud of his heritage, culture and traditions. He also believed that descendants of the Spanish colonizers of New Mexico and Pueblo Indians had much in common, most notably the Matachines heritage. Several pueblos have Matachine dancers, as do New Mexico Hispanic towns and villages. This ancient Spanish colonial dance is performed in several Indian pueblos, most notably Jemez, Taos, Ohkay Owingeh, San Ildefonso, Picuris, Santa Clara,

San Juan and Tortugas, as well as others. Ironically, many of these pueblos participated in the rebellion against the Spanish in 1680, as Dr. Sando noted. He also emphasized that traditional gifts from both cultures were shared and continue to be shared to the present day. Both cultures also share the tradition of fiestas. Dr. Sando said:

> *Indians have been putting on fiestas since the 16th century when missionaries assigned each of the pueblos a patron saint. It is in honor of the saints that the dances are performed. No budget is required, since there is no purchasing of costumes, which are handwoven and handmade by the Indians themselves. Neither do the dances demand remuneration. Committees are uncalled for, since most members of the villages habitually take part in the program in which they are most capable, that is, in dancing or in singing or in beating of the drums.*

It is interesting to note that in most pueblos that are still extant, mission churches constructed during the Spanish colonial period have been restored. Even churches that were almost destroyed during the 1680 rebellion have been painstakingly rebuilt and the exterior walls patiently replastered with mud. The centerpiece of Indian pueblos and pre-territorial Spanish villages are churches, with some dating to the seventeenth and eighteenth centuries. These places of worship were dedicated to certain saints of the Catholic Church or to Mary, the mother of Christ, as Dr. Sando noted. Examples at Indian villages include the following: a mission church at Zuni Pueblo dedicated to Nuestra Señora de la Candelaria (Our Lady of Light); Mission San Estevan del Rey (Saint Steven of the King) at Acoma; San Gerónimo Mission (Saint Jerome) at Taos; San Lorenzo Mission (Saint Lawrence) at Picuris Pueblo; San José de la Laguna (Saint Joseph of the Lagoon) at Laguna Pueblo; San Felipe (Saint Philip) at San Felipe Pueblo; Santa Clara (Saint Claire) at Santa Clara Pueblo; and Mission San Agustín de la Isleta (Saint Augustine of the Little Island) at Isleta Pueblo. This pueblo was at one time encircled by the waters of the Rio Grande River. This church was built in 1612, partially destroyed in 1680 and rebuilt in 1718. It is the burial site of Fray Juan de Padilla, who is attributed with many miraculous appearances before and after Native dances. The mission church at Acoma escaped harm during the Pueblo Indian revolt and is recognized as the oldest standing church in the United States. It is registered as a National Historic Landmark.

Jemez Pueblo performs what is called the Matachine Dance on December 12 in honor of Nuestra Señora de Guadalupe (Our Lady of Guadalupe).

This popular feast day in North America commemorates the miraculous appearances of Mary to the Indian Juan Diego on the hills of Tepeyac near Mexico City in 1531. She is venerated as the "Empress of the Americas." Other New Mexico Pueblo Indian villages that perform the Matachine Dance include San Juan, San Ildefonso, Picuris, Tortugas and Santa Clara. In 1920, Cochiti Pueblo Indian dancers performed Matachine Dances at the Fiesta de Santa Fe to enthusiastic crowds.

6

TRAILS TRAVERSED
WITH SONG AND DANCE

El Camino Real de Tierra Adentro (the Royal Highway of the Interior North) was a principal trade route from Mexico City, la Nueva España (New Spain), with various branches that ran all the way to Santa Fe. Manufactured goods were imported and exported to the capital city of New Mexico Territory, which included Arizona, Nevada, parts of Colorado, Texas and California. Goods taken to be sold in New Mexico from Mexico included books, musical instruments and dance manuals. During the lifetime of El Camino Real, from approximately 1598 until the nineteenth century, Spanish Franciscan priests who traveled the route took Latin songbooks with them to mission churches. Resident Native Americans and Spanish colonists learned Latin music and how to sing Latin church songs. Other influences included the Spanish Trail to California and the Santa Fe Trail, established around 1825 to and from Independence, Missouri. These trails further stimulated and nourished trade into New Mexico. The National Park Service maintains and administers several federally recognized Spanish colonial trails and roads. The Don Juan Bautista de Anza National Historic Trail into California is of particular interest. It is also recognized as a National Millennium Trail.

On August 24, 1777, Captain Juan Bautista de Anza Bezerra Nieto (1736–1788) was appointed governor of the Province of New Mexico by the viceroy of Nueva España, who was stationed in Mexico City. The new governor already had a very distinguished career. In 1752, de Anza, who came from a notable Spanish military family, enlisted to serve at the Presidio

Above: Rosalinda Pacheco (*left*) performs with a group of students from Escuela de Tierra Adentro in downtown Albuquerque. *Courtesy Rosalinda Pacheco*.

Left: Performance artist Rosalía de Aragón sings folkloric traditional songs at cultural centers, museums and public events in New Mexico and out of state.

de las Fronteras in the northeastern section of the Mexican state of Sonora. Here, the young soldier gained experience with the troops dealing with the Apache and other warring tribes on the Spanish borderlands. He quickly rose in rank to captain due to his prowess and courage in battle. Captain de Anza proposed an expedition into Las Californias (the present state of California). The written proposal was submitted to the viceroy of La Nueva España at the governmental center in Mexico City. His request was to explore and seek sites for presidio military forts, settlements and missions. During this time, the Internal Province of California was sparsely settled, with little Spanish control.

The king of Spain approved the expedition. Captain de Anza succeeded in several accomplishments, leading a Spanish overland expedition in 1769. He established the Presidio of San Diego. He was also the second European, after Englishman Sir Francis Drake, to see San Francisco Bay. Juan Bautista de Anza was given the rank of lieutenant colonel on October 2, 1774. On another journey, which began on October 23, 1775, de Anza led colonists and located sites for presidios and settlements in San Gabriel, Monterey, San José, Los Ángeles and San Francisco. On his return trip, the viceroy further awarded de Anza with the governorship of New Mexico. This was considered a great reward, bestowed on de Anza for his outstanding performance. Governor de Anza would serve for ten years in Santa Fe and attain recognition that has been celebrated with a historical folk play and a multitude of activities.

Governor Juan Bautista de Anza never gave up seeking a more direct trade route to California and further colonization of that area. He administered the vast New Mexico Territory that included unknown and unexplored lands. This was the Reino de Nuevo Mexico (the Kingdom of New Mexico). He attempted to maintain control by his command of the Presidio de la Santa Fe de San Francisco de Asís and its military garrison. It is interesting to note that before de Anza's time, preceding a Pueblo Indian revolt in 1680, Native American leaders were inspired by the desire to return to the days and ways of old. They spoke to one another about how good everything had been before the Spanish settlers arrived. Some of the elders blamed the colonists for severe droughts, dwindling game to hunt and failing crops.

A revolt ensued from most of the Pueblos. The Indians sought to destroy anything the Spanish had introduced, such as horses, livestock and building and farming implements. By 1692, nothing had changed for the better. In fact, the Pueblo Indians were at the mercy of warring tribes such as the Apache, Navajo and Comanche. This had been the situation for centuries before the Spanish arrived. The Spanish government in Santa Fe, including Governor Don Diego de Vargas and other governors, sought to protect both the Spanish villagers and Pueblo Indian settlements. Ceaseless attacks on peaceful settlements were an enduring problem that needed to be solved.

The huge Comanche tribe was wreaking havoc over a large area of New Mexico Territory at the time de Anza took over the governorship. This militant group of Indians was freely attacking Pueblo and Spanish settlements alike. They kidnapped women and children for a lucrative slave trade in which the captives were bartered for or sold to other tribes. Horses were stolen, and anything and everything of value was taken by force. This included foodstuffs and leather products. In October 1768, five hundred Comanche attacked the Spanish settlement of Ojo Caliente. The governor faced a vexing problem: how to pacify New Mexico. The Comanche controlled the Great Plains, most of Colorado and northern New Mexico. They consistently struck Taos and Pueblo Indian settlements at will. Governor de Anza had already served as commander of the Tubac Presidio in Arizona, New Mexico Territory. In Santa Fe, he now commanded a much larger presidio with a contingent of *caballería* (horse-mounted troops), *tropa ligera* (a rapid force), *tropa de cuero* (troops armed with heavy coats of leather armor, leather shields and iron-tipped lances), *soldados* (regular soldiers), a drum corps, fifers, a color guard and chaplains. There was also a large militia stationed in Santa Cruz de la Cañada and militias at Alburquerque and Tomé. After meeting with his officers, Governor de Anza devised a battle plan. In 1779, he traveled hundreds of miles with eight hundred heavily armed men with muskets, pistols, short swords, sabers and 2,500 horses, through Colorado and across the Arkansas River.

De Anza struck behind enemy lines, catching Comanche chief Cuerno Verde off guard with continuous volleys from their weapons. The Comanche scattered, then regrouped. The Indians had stolen horses, iron-tipped arrows and iron hatchets. Comanche warriors were also a recognized and formidable fighting force, well trained, merciless and fierce in combat. The Comanche leader wore a distinctive feather headdress with a large green horn. They, along with the Apache, Arapaho, Navajo and other tribes, had terrorized the sedentary Pueblo Indians. It is written that Cuerno Verde and fifty of his best warriors rode into a ravine and were trapped. They were all killed. Governor de Anza succeeded in negotiating peace with the Comanche. He and his force rode back triumphantly to the capital of Santa Fe. The brave Presidio soldiers were the pride of the residents. One courageous soldier was Antonio Xavier Madrid. Lieutenant Colonel and Governor de Anza signed his enlistment papers on January 4, 1768. He was the son of Santa Fe Presidio veteran Cristóbal Madrid, who died in 1765 and was buried in the San Miguel Church. Described as "five feet one inch in height, swarthy complexion, black hair and eyes," Madrid was typical of his fellow soldiers. His wife was Teodora Apolonia Valdez y Bustos.

On returning to the capital city, Governor de Anza set his sights on a peace settlement with the Hopi Indians of Arizona. He succeeded once again. Then, in 1779, the intrepid governor sought a trade route from Santa Fe to Sonora, in Mexico. On his famous Sonora Expedition, de Anza took along many Santa Fe Presidio soldiers, including Antonio Xavier Madrid; mapmaker Bernardo Miera y Pacheco, who had enlisted on January 11, 1779; and José Campo Redondo, who had enlisted on March 29, 1777, and who became an *alcalde* (mayor) in Santa Fe. Of note, Madrid and his compatriots donated funds from their soldiers' pay in support of the American Revolution. He died in 1813 and was buried at the military chapel of Our Lady of the Light, La Castrense, in Santa Fe. In his last will and testament, Antonio Xavier Madrid left his musket, blue uniform, boots and spurs and leather shield to his son José Antonio Madrid. Antonio Xavier served the Santa Fe Presidio from 1768 to 1792. Governor Juan Bautista de Anza served as governor of New Mexico from 1777 until 1787.

A New Mexico Presidio soldier memorialized the battle. A drama meant to be performed out of doors, it is called *Los Comanches*. It is believed to have been written at the end of the eighteenth century or early in the nineteenth century. One stanza emphatically states:

Soy peñasco en valentía,
En bríos y en fortaleza.
Esas locas valentías
Son criadas de la soberbia.

I am a tree of valor,
In strength and fortitude,
In reckless valiant acts
Which rise from arrogance.

Most of the dialogue takes place between Don Carlos Fernández and Cuerno Verde. In fact, Fernández says,

Siempre soy Carlos Fernández
Por el mar y por la tierra,
Y para probar tu brío
Voy a hacer junta de Guerra.

I am always Carlos Fernández
By the sea and on land,
And to test your fire
I will make enjoined War.

In examining volunteer records of the period, we find a Carlos (Xiraldo) Fernández who enlisted at the Santa Fe Presidio on January 5, 1779. Fernández, the protagonist in the drama, says he is already advanced in age. The Presidio soldier is listed as a military mapmaker with a distinguished record. He may have been considered old compared to others in the Spanish service. Regardless of who composed the drama and where it was first staged, it celebrated Governor de Anza's victory in New Mexico for posterity. The pacification of the huge Comanche tribe opened trade among Spanish traders, who were called Comancheros, the Indians and eventually American fur trappers and others. Trade fairs took place in Taos, Santa Fe and other locations in New Mexico Territory. This meant the proliferation of what Americans entering the territory would call *fandangos* (dances), using a general term.

The fur trade into Taos, New Mexico, included American fur traders, some of whom entertained themselves by playing the fiddle and singing. This was also the case with American travelers and traders in Santa Fe. New songs were brought to the area. "The Muleteer Dance" was introduced in 1838, "Leather Breeches" appeared in 1840, "Buffalo Girls" also in 1840 and "Old Dan Tucker" was played by 1843. "Durang's Hornpipe" and "Fisher's Hornpipe" appeared at an unknown

When it comes to fiestas, girls and women wear their finest dresses, replete with prized jewelry. Men were not outdone. This cavalier from around 1940 was ready.

date. "Devils Dream" and "Carry Me Back to Old Virginny" were played in New Mexico around the time of the Mexican-American War, along with "Oh! Susanna." New Mexico musicians learned from early American musicians, and vice versa. There were trade fests and what Americans called "fandangos," referring to New Mexico dances in general, not realizing that this was a particular dance. During and after the Civil War, "Arkansas Traveler," "Soldiers Joy" and "Silver Legs" were learned and played by New Mexico musicians.

Musical instruments steadily trickled in, including organs (for churches) and harps. Guitars and violins were also brought in from the East, although they were produced locally. Accordions and mandolins also appeared. In 1850, newly assigned Bishop Jean Baptiste Lamy helped to alter the New Mexican landscape. After a short time, Lamy brought in the French religious order of the Sisters of Loretto and French priests. In this way, French culture was also introduced.

The American Civil War further impacted music and dance in New Mexico Territory. Some New Mexico Union volunteers could play the drum, and they learned how to play the bugle and fifes. Before the war, New Mexico musicians learned to read musical notes and purchased printed musical compositions brought in on the Santa Fe Trail as early as 1830. Of particular note was the Union volunteer Inocencio Martínez from Taos. He was the nephew of the famous Padre Don Antonio José Martínez, New Mexico's folk-hero priest who was a defender of Native Americans and a proponent of civil rights and equal justice. Inocencio, along with other buglers and drummers, helped lead the New Mexico Union forces into battles. One of these battles would determine the fate of New Mexico Territory and Colorado and keep them from falling into the hands of the Confederacy. Inocencio, as did other American musicians of little note, led forces by playing drum rolls, singing, playing the trumpet at dawn and performing "Taps" for soldiers who had died. Higinio Cruz played and sang "El Cinco de Mayo" ("The Fifth of May"), commemorating Mexico's defeat of the French on May 5, 1865.

Juan Casados from Tomé, New Mexico, played *valses*, waltzes and *cunas*. In his short "Musical History of New Mexico," Inocencio Martínez mentioned other musicians who were his contemporaries, including Don Antonio José Ortiz, who played and sang "Dance of the Eagle" in 1821 about the independence of Mexico; "Jota de California," performed and sung by Don Tomas Lucero in 1841; and "El Talión," played by Policarpio Martínez in 1841. Inocencio Martínez also wrote of Hilario Sandoval, Mario Bibian, the

Left: Village youth learned intricate dances from older members of the communities. These girls perform the colonial dance La Jota Aragonesa for viewers around 1930.

Below: Las Fiestas have commonly featured Spanish colonial folk dancing. An admiring crowd, circa 1930s, is amazed by the girl's movements.

Matachine dancers are traditional during ceremonies in New Mexico villages and Indian pueblos such as Jemez Pueblo and Picuris Pueblo. This is a cross-cultural celebration.

Los Pandos Band; Quirino Ocaña, performed Cotillones, in 1841. Don Luis Baca, from Limitar, New Mexico, played and sang military Union songs in 1861. Martínez also mentioned La Contradanza Francesa, the French Counterdance.

Martínez traveled throughout New Mexico, playing with other local musicians and performing pieces they learned from travelers on the Santa Fe Trail and other trails. There is now a great deal of interest in preserving this musical heritage for future generations.

Herman J. Martínez, executive director of Hilos Culturales Inc., and his wife, Patricia, have strived to preserve the lifeways of New Mexico and Colorado in various ways. They help to produce *El Alba Magazine*, which features stories about those making a difference in the arts by continuing Rio Grande heritage. Hilos Culturales, which translates to "cultural threads," promotes the continuance of dances such as *valse*, polka, *chotis* and *varsoviana*. Herman and Patricia both extend projects by staging concerts, conducting seminars and hosting dialogue about the early agrarian folk culture along the San Luis Valley in Colorado and along the Rio Grande Valley in New Mexico, all through the Hilos Culturales Institute. Herman and Patricia Martínez are the driving forces touching lives throughout Hispanic communities. They both affirm:

> *Music, dance, and the visual arts preserve and connect our early rhythms of life through the works of creative and talented individuals. Live folk music and folk dance expresses the sentiments and nostalgia which is rooted in the past. Its context also appears in the present through innovation which took and takes place and is currently continued in the communities. Articles and videos feature cultural mosaics of traditional and popular music and dance performed by preservers of the culture. We also have the Premio Hilos Culturales Award that recognizes outstanding individuals that are at the forefront each and every day.*

Charles Aguilar from Bernalillo, whose family has been involved with the Matachine dancers and musicians for generations, is one of those recognized, as is Antonia Apodaca from Las Vegas, New Mexico. At one time, she performed with her accordion and sang traditional songs with the widely acclaimed group Bayou Seco.

PART II

GEMS OF TRADITION

7

SPIRITUAL FIESTA MYSTIQUE

Former ambassador to Spain Edward L. Romero has always been proud of being a descendant of the early colonizers in New Mexico. He states that he has the distinction of descending from Bartolomé Romero, who settled in 1598, and Baltazar Romero, an early founder of Albuquerque in 1706. He says:

I grew up in this culture. This is what made me, who I became, and who I am today. My family was always involved in the church. There are many things one does not ever forget. For example, there was a festival in New Mexico called Epifanía, the Epiphany. This celebrated the Magi, or the Three Kings traveling from the East from Jerusalem in search of the birth of Jesus Christ. They reached Belen, or Bethlehem, by following a luminous star. Belen, New Mexico, was named by the early Spanish in commemoration of this momentous event. Along with the early tradition of celebrating Three Kings in New Mexico with gifts, foods, and song, by recognizing that the Holy Infant Jesus who was presented with the gifts of gold, frankincense and myrrh, there was another very old custom.

During this holiday, there was a blessing of the homes with Holy Water by the village priest in memory of Christ's blessing by John the Baptist. A group of musicians with guitars, violins, and mandolins always went along playing for a large group of area residents singing our old favorite songs in Spanish. At each home blessed, special foods and delicious pastries were prepared. Another tradition that was an old part of this heritage was that

A mother or grandmother made similar grand outfits before the turn of the century for the boys prior to the Las Vegas, New Mexico fiestas.

anyone in the village who had been baptized with the named Manuel, or Manuela after Emanuel, even if it was a middle name, received a special honor. Of course, there were many Manueles and Manuelas. Also, there were many that were named Juan (John), since San Juan Bautista was a favorite saint in New Mexico. Special pastries that were prepared at the welcoming homes were empanaditas, and bizcochitos. I never forget this. It was so much fun for all of us.

Ed Romero from Albuquerque received La Gran Cruz de Isabella la Católica (the Grand Cross of Queen Isabella the Catholic) from the king and queen of Spain. As a board member and founder of the Congressional

Frances Lujan has developed and directed De Oro Productions, including *Los Bailadores de Oro*, *Los Tapatios* and *Ballet En Fuego*. *Courtesy Frances Lujan.*

Hispanic Caucus Institute in Washington, D.C., former ambassador Romero has helped increase opportunities for the Hispanic/Latino community. Each year, CHCI spearheads and hosts a week of Hispanic leadership and celebration that begins and promotes National Hispanic Heritage Month in the United States. They host an Annual Hispanic Awards Gala. He says, "A mí nunca se me olvida, I never forget our spiritual fiestas. These were always such happy events of coming together, sharing, singing, and so much happiness."

One of the most significant annual events with a long history that takes place throughout New Mexico and celebrates National Hispanic Heritage is the San Isidro Fiesta, from around May 10 to the saint's feast day on May 15. This has been taking place since the early Spanish colonial period and dates to years before that to Spain. San Isidro Labrador (Saint Isidore the Ploughman) is the patron saint of Madrid and a patron saint of Spain. In fact, in Spain, this famous Roman Catholic saint is so highly regarded that there are parades and a multitude of festivities and holiday foods to honor him. San Isidro is the progenitor of cherishing land and water. He rose each morning in the early days of Madrid, went to church and prayed; then he and his wife, Santa María Toribia (also canonized as a saint), helped to feed the poor and hungry and care for all. San Isidro and Santa María were also a poor couple, but they graciously shared from the little they had. Miraculously, it is said, their bounty increased as they gave generously.

In New Mexico, San Isidro is the patron saint of farmers, ranchers and, of course, ploughmen. Almost from the time Spanish colonists arrived in New Mexico and after recolonization in 1692, settlers built a massive irrigation system throughout the territory. Native Americans also had an ancient irrigation system, but it was nothing like the advanced technological water system built by the Spanish that still exists in some areas today.

The colonizers brought time-tested Western ideas that had been introduced to them by the Romans, Moors and other old-world civilizations into the Iberian Peninsula. Spanish pioneers saw the land and immediately went to work digging channels in order to water and irrigate lands that were already fertile and other areas that had little or no water. Government leaders in Santa Fe saw a vital need for the Spanish colony to survive and succeed, and they addressed it.

Agriculture was the basis of not only New Mexico's Spanish colonial economy but also that of the Pueblo Indians. In time, each culture complemented the other in the effort to survive in a harsh land. In this way, a Spanish event, the fiesta, was transferred from the motherland to New Mexico. It certainly took a tremendous effort on the part of men and women to accomplish the tremendous amount of backbreaking work. Prayers and songs, such as the following to San Isidro, "Alabanza a San Isidro" ("Praises to San Isidro"), rang throughout New Mexico:

San Isidro Labrador,
Patrón de los labradores,
Que nos libre tu favor
De langostas y temblores.

Por la gran misericordia
Con que te ayudo el Señor,
Derrama paz y concordia
Entre todo Labrador.

Cuando el Señor por castigo
Nos manda mal temporal,
Con tu bondadoso abrigo
Nos vemos libres de mal.

Del ladrón acostumbrado
Que nunca teme al Señor,
Nos libres nuestro sembrado
Te pedimos por favor.

El granizo destructor
Que nos causa su daño:
Te pedimos con fervor
Tener cosecha este año.

En tus bondades confiado
Te pido de corazón
Le mandes a mi sembrado
Favores y bendición.

Adiós oh santo glorioso,
Escogido del Señor,
Hasta el año venidero,
San Isidro Labrador.

Saint Isidore the Ploughman
Patron of all farmers,
May we be delivered by your favor
From locusts and tremors.

By your great compassion
With which Our Lord helped you
Spread peace and harmony,
Among everything Ploughman.

When punished by our Lord,
And bad times come,
Cover us with your overcoat,
That we may be free from harm.

From the customary thief
Who never fears our Lord,
Keep our seedlings safe
We beg you please.

Keep away destructive hail
That causes so much harm,
We ask you with fervor,
We may harvest this year.

I confide in your kindness
I ask with all my heart
You protect all I have planted
With favors and blessing.

Goodbye, oh glorious saint,
Selected by Our Lord
Until next year,
Saint Isidore the Ploughman.

Fertile fields were ploughed, planted and cultivated. Deep ditches called *acequia madres* (mother ditches) meant to carry water from the Rio Grande and rivers to wide fields were dug. This took months of intense labor with picks, shovels and other iron tools. Then channels known as *contracequias* were also dug. These were smaller ditches attached to high canals that spread out, followed by *renajes*, other branches that carried water to the fields.

In more isolated areas such as northern New Mexico, when a river was not nearby, water was drawn from streams or from natural springs called *ojos*. This water was then transported by a system of *canoas*, dug-out cottonwood trunks sometimes placed onto wooden stilts, depending on the terrain. *Compuertas*, wood shutoffs placed on *contracequias* at intervals, helped regulate water flow. Spanish colonists also used various measures to create ponds of water for livestock and wildlife.

New Mexico santero artists carved and produced wooden images of San Isidro in the round and representations of him on retablos. He is shown wearing Spanish colonial dress with short, knee-length pants, a black, wide-brimmed hat, leggings, black shoes and a frock coat. The three-dimensional or flat bearded figure is shown with a plow pulled by one or two oxen. An angel guides the farmer and his plow. San Isidro is attributed with over one hundred miracles. The saint is invoked to protect crops from locusts, hail, floods and drought. It is generally believed that San Isidro had the special ability to find water. His image is carried out of churches dedicated to his memory in New Mexico or out of chapels in special processions. There are two communities named after the saint:

This traditional retablo painting on pine by Rosa María Calles portrays San Isidro Labrador. The saint of farmers is celebrated in both Hispanic villages and Indian pueblos.

San Isidro del Norte (St. Isidore of the North) and San Isidro del Sur (St. Isidore of the South).

The procession during the San Isidro Fiesta is led by the saints' statue carried on a litter or by a painting. A speech, the *pregón*, is given by El Pregonero, someone proclaiming the celebration of this important saint and holiday. At the chapel or church, a *función* is held. This is a festivity with a Mass given on the feast day. It includes singing and a priest's sermon. The large crowd, at times including Pueblo Indians if they do not have their own celebrations, follows the priest into the fields and the acequias for special blessings. What is requested through song and hymns is San Isidro's intervention for a bountiful harvest. In New Mexico, this is particularly requested in the fall for a fruitful harvest of chile, pinto beans, squash and corn. Members of the community clean the acequias of weeds and debris if they have not already been cleaned before the fiesta, and re-dig them. Seeds are planted in the fields, then water is slowly released as people clap and cheer. Then the real celebration begins with singing to guitars and violins and partaking of a glorious feast. In Spain and in some parts of New Mexico, participants dance the chotis. Fertile pastoral lands in New Mexico provide nourishment and ingredients for recipes and meals cherished by all. Many important fiestas take place in New Mexico throughout the year. And in December, many Fiestas de la Navidad take place. It is a month filled to the brim with celebration and joy.

An ancient narrative from the play *Los Pastores* (*The Shepherds*) has existed from time immemorial in New Mexico. It proclaims: "The Shepherds start marching towards Bethlehem, where they expect to see the Messiah lying in a manger. En la Jornada hacia Belen, on their journey towards Bethlehem they sing pastoral songs of joy, joining nature with all its inherent beauty, in praising God in their simple shepherd fashion."

In the play, also known as *La Pastorela*, mock swords clash. An angel appears wearing stiff wings. The angel thrusts up its sword in triumph, defeating someone dressed as Lucifer. It is the Archangel Michael precipitating the adoration of the Christ child in the manger. It is a medieval story transported

Ramon Juan Carlos de Aragón (*left*) and the author (*right*) portray shepherds on their way to Bethlehem following a star for the play *Los Pastores*, which is performed annually.

to New Mexico from the time of colonization. It is a dramatic cultural experience, and one of many. This is an integral part of the folklore that is presented during the Christmas season. Another is *Las Posadas* (*The Inns*). Surprised homeowners barely open a door and discover a group of travelers strongly knocking at the door. They ask,

Who comes to our door,
On such a cold wintry night?
Who is here disturbing our rest?

Those outside, playing guitars and singing, respond and implore,

Who will give us lodging?
We are such tired travelers.
We have walked forever,
And have gone through
So many roads.

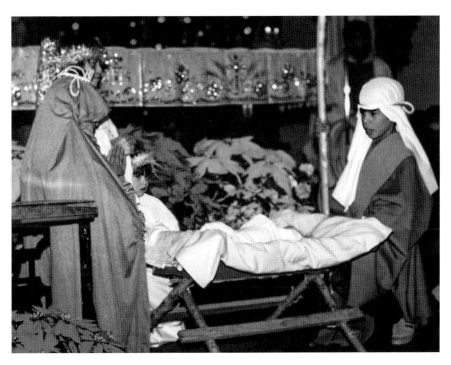

Las Posadas (*The Inns*), a popular ancient drama that follows Mary and Joseph seeking shelter, is shown with the birth of Christ at a church.

After a series of requests in Spanish for a place to rest, which are responded to by those inside the home, doors swing wide open and everyone joins in on the joy and singing. *Las Posadas* is a generations-old story about the birth of Christ as told by Saint Luke. It is recounted in the form of a nine-day novena in many homes throughout New Mexico. Every hosting family prepares their own homes with special Christmas treats, including *posole* (homemade hominy), *empanaditas* (turnovers), *bizcochitos* (special cookies), *pastelitos* (little pies), plenty of cooked red chile, *natillas* (a type of custard pudding) and *sopa* (bread pudding).

A boy is selected to play the role of Joseph, and a girl portrays Mary. Sometimes, she must ride on a donkey from house to house each night. They both wear traditional costumes stitched from bright cloth by a loving mother or grandmother. This helps to keep the tradition alive. Several individuals devote many hours to putting on the deceptively simple production. Rosa María Calles is one of many dedicated to keeping this tradition alive. In Las Vegas, New Mexico, for example, she solicited families for nearly thirty years, scheduled the village priest, arranged for guitarists and provided scripts for everyone to follow. At a final home, everyone makes space for nearly two hundred people. Happy conversations follow, with everyone enjoying a feast day with delicious foods. At times through falling snow, most of the community gathers at the church for La Misa del Gallo (Midnight Mass) on December 24 that proclaims the birth of Christ on Christmas Day.

It is interesting to note that some roles pass down from father to son or mother to daughter. Such is the case for *El Coloquio de los Pastores* (*The Conversation between the Shepherds*), *Las Apariciones de Nuestra Señora de Guadalupe* (*The Apparitions of Our Lady of Guadalupe*) and *Los Tres Reyes Magos* (*The Three Kings*). On la Noche Buena (the good night), on Christmas Eve and before, Native Americans at the pueblos and villages also celebrate. An early Spanish Franciscan priest once proclaimed:

> *The Indians celebrate the feasts of the Lord, of Our Lady and of the principal patron saints of the villages with much rejoicing and solemnity.… Along with their regular clothes they wear their bright colored feathers.… Indians perform dances and sing to the beats of drums in their tongues, celebrating their feasts.…Their songs which are heartfelt and spiritual begin at midnight in the village square, last through the night and go on throughout the next day.*

Las Posadas celebrates Christmas in New Mexico by re-creating Mary and Joseph seeking shelter before the birth of Christ. Traditions fill the holiday.

Pueblo Indians crowd into the mission churches at Christmas and stand devotedly outside if there is no more room. Midnight Mass is usually followed by ceremonial dances. In some places, brightly lit bonfires called *luminarias* light up the night sky. In some places in New Mexico, the old tradition of stacking *piñon* wood in certain ways is still done, as it has been done for centuries. As a young boy growing up in Las Vegas, New Mexico, I was fortunate to see and experience the ancient luminarias. This was at the Plaza Park in Old Las Vegas. Logs of wood were carefully placed in rectangular shapes around the park and then lit. These impressive fires illuminated the sky and burned through the night. Especially at the Indian pueblos, where heritage and traditions are retained, these luminarias provide a beautiful backdrop for ancient rituals.

In the twenty-first century, it is obviously not appropriate to build bonfires in the cities. New Mexico is unique in the entire country and in other countries for having a new type of luminaria. Someone came up with the idea of using brown paper bags for the lighting. They folded them neatly at the top, placed a trowel of sand into the bags, then inserted candles and lit

During the darkness of Christmas Eve, thousands of candles glow in paper bags called *luminarias* in New Mexico to signal the coming birth of Christ.

these up in front of houses and driveways. No one knows exactly by whom or when this was done initially. All that is known is that some ingenious person or persons arrived at the idea and that it caught on like wildfire. Some people attempt to take credit for this invention, which is used only in New Mexico and is now an integral part of Christmas tradition, along with Christmas trees, Saint Nicholas and the joyous birth of Christ. Luminarias are now part of New Mexico Spanish culture, meant to be appreciated and enjoyed by all. Thousands of luminarias glowing on Christmas Eve illuminate the skies of the state, attract tourists and are featured on the news throughout the country. Albuquerque features a Christmas tour in which thousands of people travel in vehicles with headlights turned off to simply relish and enjoy a once-in-a-lifetime experience. And they return year after year. They also return to enjoy other Christmas fiestas and foods.

8

FIESTA FOODS AND GLAD TIDINGS

¡Panza llena, corazón contento! (A full stomach leads to a happy heart!)

This ageless and well-known *dicho* (saying) from New Mexico's old proverbs pretty much sums up the people's sentiment about the state's delicious foods. This is especially so when the foods are associated with fiestas and festivals. It may be asked, "What contributes to exuberant celebrations?" Of course, one answer is entertainment in various forms. But what draws hundreds and even thousands of people to various events are food, beverages and songs. Cultural recipes are very much a part of a region's heritage.

As literary chairman of the Feria Artesana, one of the largest arts festivals in the country, held in Albuquerque, New Mexico and sponsored by the mayor's office and the City Parks and Recreation Department, one of my duties was to interview and write about those selected to be honored at the event. Stories about their lives were included in *Feria Artesana* magazine. I got to interview Fabiola Cabeza de Baca, who had a long and distinguished career. Even at an advanced age, Doña Fabiola beamed with happiness and joy when she recalled her experiences in various communities and with people around New Mexico. Fabiola Cabeza de Baca nostalgically recalled things to me as I took notes and questioned her.

First came La Marcha, the March, in which everyone took part, husbands, wives, brothers and sisters, and some daring young fellows with their

Above: Crowds gather to enjoy the food that accompanies *matanzas*. A famous one in which hundreds participate takes place annually in Belen, New Mexico. *Courtesy of Don Chávez.*

Left: Distinguished Fabiola Cabeza de Vaca provided old recipes in her *Santa Fe New Mexican* newspaper column and in a classic cookbook for various events.

sweethearts danced together. The musicians with their violins, guitars and accordions were seated on a platform. It was a beautiful sight to see the dancing feet of the women as they were lost in the fast rhythms of the polkas, schottisches, waltzes and varsovianas, and only the boots could be seen and heard. I know we have not yet found among the petroglyphs and sandstone glyphs which archaeologists have identified as circles, and have called them, "Sun Symbols" and many other pictographs, what could be representations of early food in New Mexico. Perhaps, they may in fact, represent the first tortillas made by one of the first Basket Maker Indian women. What is out there could be easily explained if we open our eyes.

When I interviewed Fabiola Cabeza de Baca, author of *We Fed Them Cactus, The Good Life, New Mexico Traditions and Food* and *Historic Cookery*, I met her at a nursing home. Doña Fabiola had a long, distinguished career in New Mexico as a home economist and an award-winning writer. She was born in 1894 on her family ranch near the village of La Liendre, close to my hometown of Las Vegas, New Mexico. She served in the Agricultural Extension Service in northern New Mexico for over thirty years. Among her many accomplishments was training extension agents in agriculture for the United Nations in Latin American countries. She beamed with joy when I said she was being featured for the Albuquerque *Feria Artesana* magazine. She had much to tell me as she smiled and recalled the past for me. Oral interview is the best way to record history.

New Mexico is a land of changes; its blue skies of morning may be the red skies of the evening. In recent years, New Mexican foods have become very popular around the world.

In New Mexico, one thinks of red chiles drying in the sun, outdoor beehive-like ovens called hornos and the adobe houses which marvelously blend in with our glorious landscape. This has all been a part of the lives of Hispanics in New Mexico, since the settlement. People drew their sustenance from the spirit and soul of this land. Each season in New Mexico has its own foods during festivities, celebrations and fiestas. For example, during Christmas, molletes (sweet rolls) are made. There are also bizcochito (anise seed cookies) [and] empanaditas, which are cut rounds of dough about three inches in diameter, filled with ground sweetened meat with raisins, and piñon nuts, folded and pinched together and then deep fried. Other foods during this period are posole, corn steamed and dried on the cob, then shelled and cooked with pork in water until tender, and

The Albuquerque International Balloon Fiesta, with approximately five hundred hot-air balloons, attracts people from all around the world. Special shapes highlight the event, along with balloon glows.

tamales, shredded cooked pork coated with a red chile paste. The pork mixture is placed over masa harina dough (a corn flour product) which has been spread over corn husks and rolled together to seal then steamed. The time of feasting is also the time of folk dramas, such as Los Pastores *and* Las Posadas.

During betrothal feasts and weddings, people ate capirotada (bread pudding), marquesotes (light sponge cakes) and other dishes such as

In every town and village, there are causes for celebrating, such as births, baptisms, confirmations and weddings. The entire community apparently showed up for a double wedding around 1920 in northern New Mexico.

The age-old process of burying a pig or lamb in a pit with embers overnight, then butchering it during festivities, is still done.

morcilla, blood from a butchered lamb made into blood pudding, or simply fried. Pretty much all of an animal is used in the preparation of New Mexico foods at various celebrations and festivities such the tongue, tripe and stomach. In some New Mexico villages, there are wild plants such as quelites (spinach), wild parsley and purslane, a prolific weed found in abundance out in fields.

In the past, traditional music was furnished by village musicians which included a violin and guitar. At weddings there was the grand march (La Marcha), La Entriega de los Novios (the release of the bride and groom and their obligations to each other as well as the community), El Vals Chiquillada (a waltz where partners exchanged verses). The bride sat on a chair in the middle of the dance floor while the groom favored her with different extemporaneous verses that could be complimentary, or even humorous. The bride responded with her own to the delight of the wedding party. There were quadrilles, schottisches and varsoviana dances enjoyed by everyone.

During Lent, people ate panocha (a sprouted wheat pudding), torrejas (egg fritters with seasoned red chile) and whole wheat tortillas. When one thinks of New Mexican foods and dishes, naturally, chile comes first with its pungent flavor, which everyone craves. Add chicos (dried green steamed corn) to cooked beans, and people's mouths water. Morcilla is blood from a butchered lamb made into delicious blood pudding. Then there were also the matanzas. An animal was cooked and roasted in a special way.

9

THE GREATEST GENERATION IMPACTS FIESTAS

New Mexicans volunteered by the thousands to join the U.S. war effort during World War II. Young men leaving to fight in Europe left a void at farms and ranches. Rubel Abeyta had to leave his guitar behind and raise his rifle. Going off to war affected many musicians, and this of course also affected fiestas. Almost every single Hispanic family in New Mexico had members who served during the war. When the men returned, they introduced new music and new dances to New Mexico celebrations. Rubel composed the following ballad, "El Corrido de los Estados Unidos" ("The Ballad of the United States"), and sang it before leaving overseas.

A los Estados Unidos,
Le compuse este corrido,
Para que se acuerden de mí,
Que Mañana me despido,
Al servicio militario,
A pelear por mi país.

…Hay que levantar las fuerzas,
Con armamento y soldados.

Quiero que el enemigo,
Oiga mi canción,
Y que la oiga por medio,
De un estallido de cañón,

Cuando las disparan,
Las tropas de la nación.

Tropas de Estados Unidos,
Como También las Aliadas,
Los tengo en mi corazón,
También en mi alma,
Que no formen traición,
Entre esta horrible guerra.

A los padres de familia,
Damos miles de gracia
Que tienen hijos allá,
A su patria dando honores,
Defendiendo su bandera,
Peleando los alemanes.

Adiós, parientes queridos,
Hermanas, primos, tíos, y tías,
Alli les encargo a mi madre,
Es el único favor que pido,
Ya me despido a la guerra,
Por los Estados Unidos.

Se despide de ustedes,
Este trovador Hispano,
Dando muchísimas gracias,
Por haberme escuchado,
Estoy listo para servirles,
Nunca me hallaran cansado,
Ofrezco mi vida a mi patria.
Ahora me voy de soldado.

To the United States,
I composed this ballad,
So that you remember me,
For tomorrow I leave,
To serve in the military
To fight for my country.

…We must build our forces.
With arms and soldiers.

I want the enemy,
To hear my song,
And to hear it,
From a cannon burst,
When it is fired,
By our nation's troops.

Troops of the United States,
As well as the Allies,
I have them in my heart,
And in my soul,
That no treason is formed
During this horrible war.

To the fathers with families,
We give many thanks,
That have sons over there,
Honoring their country,
Defending their flag,
Fighting the Germans.

Goodbye, my beloved family,
Sisters, cousins, uncles, and aunts,
I entrust you with my mother,
It's the only favor I ask,
I bid farewell. I'm off to war,
For the United States.

This Hispanic troubadour
Bids you farewell,
Giving many thanks,
For listening to me,
I'm ready to serve you,
You will never find me tired,
I offer my life for my country,
Now I'm off as a soldier.

Left: In 1941, Rubel Abeyta put aside his guitar for a firearm. He wrote "El Corrido de los Estados Unidos," a ballad about World War II. *Courtesy of Velma Salazar.*

Below: Los Abeytas, a family passing down music from one generation to the next, performed at fiestas for decades. *Courtesy of Velma Salazar.*

Around 1942, Rubel Abeyta, from the farming and ranching community of El Ojo del Caballo in northern New Mexico, was drafted into the U.S. Army along with two of his brothers. They came from a family of eleven children, six of whom were musicians who played the guitar and violin. Their parents, Don Felipe Abeyta, and Laura Martínez de Abeyta, stimulated singing and the playing of musical instruments in the family. This was a longstanding tradition in other families in the community. As a musical group, the Abeyta family played traditional folk music for baptisms, weddings, feast days, holidays and fiestas.

After the Japanese attack on Pearl Harbor in 1941, a universal patriotic spirit swept into New Mexico and the rest of the country. Rubel then penned his ballad at the outset of American involvement in the war. In Las Vegas, New Mexico, a great deal of excitement filled the air when KFUN radio first began broadcasting in the northern part of the state. The event took place on Christmas Day 1941. Many went out and purchased battery-operated radios to listen to music and hear the news. President Franklin D. Roosevelt's famous speech was heard around town. Rubel Abeyta, with guitar in hand, introduced his ballad to the world at KFUN Radio along with another song he wrote, "La Despidida" ("The Farewell"). His touching composition in honor of American soldiers who would be fighting and dying in World War II exemplified what took place in New Mexico at the outset of the war.

Joseph Krumgold received the Newbery Medal for his book ...And Now Miguel in 1954. In the book, he wrote about a fast-disappearing agrarian way of life in New Mexico that was vastly impacted by events in Europe during the war. What was taking place certainly inspired his award-winning novel when the United States joined the war.

Krumgold's historical fiction novel revolves around Miguel Chávez, a twelve-year-old boy growing up in northern New Mexico. His older brother Gabriel was off to fight for his country in World War II. Miguel believed he had an opportunity to join the other men sheepherding in the area of the Sangre de Cristo Mountain range. The young boy participated in the farm life of his home by helping with chores. He loved lambing time, when the lambs were born, and he helped care for them and assisted in searching for lost sheep. He also saw the men who came from around the community to help with the shearing. Miguel Chávez often prayed to San Isidro Labrador, the patron saint of farmers, to help him realize his dream. He longed to join the adult males and that they would notice that he could do things with the best of them. His older brother also prayed, but it was to have the opportunity to experience the rest of the world far from his isolated life in New Mexico. The wishes and dreams of both came true, but not in the ways they expected.

Excitement filled the air in New Mexico as thousands of Hispanics joined in the war effort to liberate Europe. World War II affected New Mexico fiestas, as both men and women sought to help. Camp Luna near Las Vegas, New Mexico, and other areas in the state were training centers for troops. Enthusiasm reached new heights. Men going off to war affected nearly every Hispanic family. An inordinate number of New Mexican Hispanic soldiers were tortured by the Japanese in the Philippine Islands, and many died on the infamous Bataan Death March. Those who survived and returned home helped create a melting pot of fun and gaiety at community events. There was resilience and innovation, with new dances such as the Jitterbug. Later, there were "sock hops" for the youth that included dance contests. It isn't generally known that Albuquerque and New Mexico also experienced the zoot suit movement of the 1940s. Hispanic youth wore the notorious zoot suit (long sports coat, wide pants cuffed at the ankle) and sometimes a wide hat and a dangling chain. Zoot suiters crashed fiesta dances, and rock 'n' roll ruled in the 1950s. This was an additional amalgamation of New Mexico fiestas.

10

FIESTAS COMING OF AGE

Best-selling author Rudolfo Anaya, in his famous coming-of-age book *Bless Me, Ultima*, nostalgically wrote: "It's been a long time since Ultima left us and yet it seems like just yesterday. I remember my father's advice, 'Ay, every generation, every man is a part of his past. He can reform the materials, make something new.'"

In 1960, New Mexico celebrated the 350th anniversary of the founding of Santa Fe with fiestas, proclamations and celebrations. Governor John Burroughs wrote words praising this glorious history: "The three hundred and fiftieth anniversary of La Villa Real de Santa Fe de San Francisco de Asis is an event of national as well as local significance. The city of Santa Fe has achieved that rare, almost unique blending of past, present, and future, just as it has achieved to a rare degree, a happy commingling of peoples, customs, and cultures."

The governor's proclamation served to protect and honor a long history in the country. Mayor Leo T. Murphy added:

The 350th Anniversary of the founding of Santa Fe is a...source of inspiration to our residents to nurture and protect a tradition of honest labor, of sacrifice to achieve a cherished objective, and of sufficient time out from the rigors of daily toil to savor the special bouquet of life in Santa Fe....I extend a cordial invitation to visit us at the earliest opportunity to share our enjoyment of the City Different, its history, its unique charm and its incomparable climate."

Vignette
Adapted and Directed by Rosa Maria Calles

THE BIG READ
Rudolfo Anaya's "Bless Me, Ultima"

Saturday, October 6th, 2007
National Hispanic Cultural Center
Bank of America Theater
6:00 pm

The National Endowment for the Arts has sponsored a month-long series of activities in Bernalillo County to promote literacy and reading for pleasure.

The National Endowment for the Arts highlighted the dramatic stage adaptation of Rudolfo Anaya's *Bless Me, Ultima*, written and directed by distinguished playwright Rosa María Calles.

Left: Enrique Jesús de Aragón played the lead role of Antonio Marés y Luna for the adaptation of *Bless Me, Ultima*. Anaya called him "fantastic and real!"

Right: Fiesta time means dressing up, going with family and friends and having fun. Here, Marisa Rodriguez is out at the Espanola Fiestas, prepared for the entertainment.

Fiesta attire was required, including Spanish costumes, traditional Indian dress and clothing reflecting the American territorial period. Dr. José-Pablo García, who taught at Lydia Patterson Institute in El Paso, Texas, and was the distinguished department head of the music department at New Mexico Highlands University in Las Vegas, New Mexico, once profoundly stated: "When one goes to fiestas and listens to the Orquesta Típica, traditional musicians, play our beloved Corridos, Rancheras, Polkas, Valses, Cotilos, and El Chotis, we are letting the music express the innermost elements of our very soul. At the same time, we are putting ourselves in communion and harmony with the rest of the Hispanic world which is forming a closely-knit family which as time goes on, speaks more and more with one Latino voice."

The current celebration of Cinco de Mayo in New Mexico and other areas is a manifestation of the words expressed so eloquently many times by Dr. García. In fact, he was one of those instrumental in founding this event in the state.

During the American Civil War, France found an opportunity to invade the Republic of Mexico. Meanwhile, the Union and the Confederacy were

Los Bailadores de Oro, with the women displaying their fans. Handheld fans, *abanicos fandango*, have been used in dance since the Spanish colonial era. *Courtesy of Frances Lujan.*

embroiled in a bitter war. French troops and the French navy launched a massive assault on Mexico and took over the capital. Napoleon III of France installed Austro-Hungarian Ferdinand Maximilian von Hapsburg as emperor of Mexico, and his wife, Carlota, became empress. If one could say something good came from this, it would be that Carlota most probably had a very sincere love for the Mexican people. Her affection traveled along El Camino Real and into New Mexico Territory. French waltzes, perhaps even the polka and other dances, and music and musical instruments were imported into Santa Fe and became an integral part of New Mexico folk dance, folk culture and folk music.

The victory of Mexican forces over the French army at Puebla in 1862 gave birth to the holiday called Cinco de Mayo. The famous battle took place on May 5, 1862. The historic battle is depicted in a folk play in many places in Mexico. It is now a cultural celebration that has caught on in the United States, with parades and floats in California, among other places. Folkloric dances from Spain and Mexico, including flamenco and traditional dances from various Mexican states, are also part of the celebration. It is no longer simply a Mexican American celebration, but an American holiday. National marketing campaigns have ensured that Cinco de Mayo fiesta foods and drinks as well as *papel picado* (paper flower making) and carnival rides reflect common cultural pride for one and all.

11

FIESTAS MEMORIES AND RESILIENCE

L as Vegas, New Mexico native Dr. Mari-Luci Jaramillo, former ambassador to Honduras who coauthored the book *Sacred Seeds: A Girl, Her Abuelos, and the Heart of Northern New Mexico*, never forgot her upbringing, hardships and roots.

I was the first Hispanic to serve as a United States ambassador. Growing up, my family lived in Old Town. My father had a shoe repair business on Bridge Street. It was always hard making ends meet. But there are past experiences I will never forget. I wanted to go to college, so I saved every penny I earned. I shined shoes at my father's shop after school. I also worked at the Parachute Factory by the plaza park. During World War II I worked with other women knitting woolen sweaters for the soldiers. I got an award for knitting the quickest and making the most sweaters. One of the things that made the most impression on me was going with my family to mass at the Our Lady of Sorrows church and participating in the church fiestas. It was such great fun for all of us. Our neighbors back then treated us like we were part of family so their doors were always open, and we could go in and eat, play games, and even dance. We were all so blessed. I think the way I grew up in Vegas and all the help I received when I attended Highland University contributed to my getting my Bachelors' Degree, my Masters, and eventually my Doctorate. I was also greatly supported at the University

of New Mexico where I was involved in Latin American Studies. I did presentations in bilingual education even back in my hometown. No one ever forgot me there. I didn't leave Las Vegas fiestas either. I always went back to see my family and friends and continued to experience the fun and the joy of the old days.

John B. Mondragón and Ernest S. Stapleton coauthored *Public Education in New Mexico*. They wrote in the chapter "La Llorona Bridges History and Cultures":

Instructional materials used in New Mexican schools did not always celebrate our wondrous quadra-cultural history. The curricula represented mostly traditional "American" history with scant references to the rich medley of New Mexicans who forged this state's history. Since the 1960's, we have observed the inclusion of some fascinating material, not the least of which has been the story of "La Llorona, the Wailing Woman," whose travails have been used to alert children, parents, and communities to the dangers of the ditches in New Mexico. Convoluted as the story may be about how La Llorona met her demise, it is classic folklore in New Mexico, Cuba, Central America, and South America. A heralded version is the wondrous stage play, Cuento de La Llorona Tale of the Wailing Woman, by Rosa María Calles, performed on many stages, such as the Lensic Theater in Santa Fe, the Macey Theater, the National Hispanic Cultural Center, and the Ricardo Montalban Theater in Hollywood, California, with sponsorship at this Los Ángeles venue by Walt Disney Studios. Calles'

Opposite: Linda Dulcinea de Aragón (*second from left*) joyously rehearses with the dance group "Baila! Baila!" prior to a performance at the Las Vegas fiestas.

Above: Our Lady of Sorrows parish council in Las Vegas, New Mexico, selected Rosa María Calles's painting *La Función* as the 100th fiesta anniversary poster.

version offers an intriguing story of star-crossed lovers and peasants versus patrones (upper class familias).....New Mexico's schools at all levels can today mine a rich trove of indigenous curricular materials....The treasure trove of folk culture inspired by fiestas such as in my original hometown of Socorro not only brings back wonderful memories, but of our participation in joyous events.

In my life I was very lucky to have known and visited with people who came to influence my life and career. There was Jesusita Aragón. She was "La Partera," the famous midwife who helped hundreds of infants come into this world. She glowed with pride about her life's work and reminisced about the old days. Fabiola Cabeza de Baca Gilbert spoke of the evolution of her acclaimed life and career, as did Sabine Ulibarri, who grew up in Tierra Amarilla. Concha Ortiz y Pino de Kleven lovingly called me "El Barbón," "the bearded one," since I had a beard as soon as I could grow one. Concha was also renowned and gifted in New Mexico Hispano culture and tradition, as was Miguel Encinias, who strongly supported me and my efforts. Fray Angélico Chávez was both a relative and a mentor, as was Tibo Chávez, who gave me a wealth of knowledge about *los remedios de la gente* ("the home remedies of our people"). Civil rights leader Reies López Tijerina pushed me into an incredible journey with his profound passion about stolen lands. I closely interacted with Al "Hurricane" Sánchez, a member of the New Mexico Air National Guard, dubbed "The Enchilada Air Force," and with his brothers Baby Gaby and Tiny Morrie. They always called me up to dance onstage when they played "The Funky Chicken" at their Far West nightclub in Albuquerque. I was fortunate to meet their mother, Bennie Sánchez, executive director of Hurricane Records. We joked about being related through my mother. She provided me with advice that was much appreciated. Rudolfo Anaya was the counselor at Valley High School when I was a student there, and he was then a counselor at the University of Albuquerque, from which I graduated after high school. I served as the activities vice-president of the student senate at U of A. Rudolfo and I had a lifelong friendship. He told me, "I have always followed your writing." I also followed his very successful career. Roberto Mondragón was a DJ at the KABQ Spanish radio station. When he served as lieutenant governor and later became a popular singer, we communicated often. He and Georgia Roybal, Roberto's partner in *Aspectos Culturales*, a marvelous publication in support of New Mexico Hispano history, played an important part in my career. Ana Pacheco, with her periodical *La Herencia: The Heritage & History*

Left: Chautauqua performer Rosalía de Aragón travels throughout New Mexico and out of state, performing as the legendary ghost La Llorona at festivals.

Below: In 1946, Adolfo Calles returned home to Tomé from World War II in time for the Passion Play, carrying the image of Christ in the Vía Crucis.

That Is New Mexico, inspired everyone who read it. Don Pedro Ribera Ortega was a dear friend. He was both a companion and an associate, as was Juan José Peña, a fellow student in high school. Roberto Griego and I were pals, and I followed his gigs whenever he played his music. Other entertainers I associated with included Joe Bravo.

As a youth, I was captivated and nurtured by my mother's passion for her early upbringing. María Cleofas Sánchez de Aragón was born in the little mountain village of Peñasco Blanco in 1915. The influenza epidemic of 1918 had taken many lives in New Mexico, but those living in the isolated mountain villages of the north were not hit as hard by this terrible epidemic. Her father was Don Filimon Sánchez, and her mother was Pablita Romero de Sánchez. Filimon was a hermano and an elder member of the Penitente Brotherhood. Pablita belonged to Las Carmelitas, the complementary lay women's order. Both orders were centuries old in New Mexico, and both dealt with the Passion sufferings of Jesus Christ, the Nazarene, on his Vía Crucis, and with his most sorrowful mother, Mary.

Recounting her childhood and youth, my mother demonstrated a profound fluency in her native language of Spanish. She always said, "Debes de saber tu propia idioma" ("You must know your own language"). And while communicating this to me in her endeared language, she glowingly spoke about her incredible journey from the past to the present. I never forget about her pride and her heartfelt memories.

> *I grew up in a time when we had dirt floors in our adobe home. I never forget when I had to sweep sheep's blood on the hard packed floor. My sisters and I had already spent time sweeping all the dust off the floors, every single speck of dust until it was all clean. Then we had to carry the sheep's blood in. Our father had butchered some lambs, and they had collected the blood. It was brought to me and my sisters to use on our floors. After sweeping, the floors looked like cement. These floors of dirt lasted for months this way. As little girls, we followed our mother up into the hills to collect Hierba de la Escoba, a plant which had stems we used to make our own brooms.*
>
> *I have so many beautiful memories. My youth was filled with such joy and happiness. Corn was gathered and piled up high in one of our rooms. My sisters and I shucked the corn. This took hours. We saved some corn shucks and corn leaves to make our dolls. We decorated our dolls. They were so pretty. Our brothers helped our father with mending fences and caring for the livestock that provided us with meat, and goats we milked for*

cheese. We also gathered roots of the amole plant to make shampoo, and we picked other plants such as Osha and plumajillo, for remedios, remedies for illness, cuts and scrapes. The medicinal herbs helped us pull through during the terrible epidemic.

When someone did die, my brothers helped my father and others make the coffins out of pine. The girls helped the women dress up the coffins with cloth. We recycled everything so each and every item served a purpose in life, and in death. We sang our hearts out at the funerals. Teníamos canticos y canciones para todo. We had canticles and songs for every occasion.

It was a good life. We had everything. For what we didn't have, all families went out in teams of wagons to the Llano, the plains, to trade. We had fruit trees with apples. Neighbors had peaches. Others had sugar beets, vegetables, sugar, salt. We also took tins of lard because we had pigs. By the time we returned home my family had everything. We dried fruit, made jerky, and canned all else to help us make it through the

Estevan Pacheco (*center*) smiles as he is surrounded by girls. They are ready, willing and anxious to perform at fiestas.

seasons. Back before this some of our ancestors were Ciboleros, those of our men that went out hunting for cíbolos (buffalo), and they also traded with the Comanche Indians.

I can say we worked from sunup until sundown. But those were the happy days. We used oil lamps. We had wood burning stoves. We had a well for water. We all took turns bathing in a metal tub after the water was warmed up. We had plenty to eat and we were all happy. We had no bills to pay. My father only paid a small tax for the property we owned to the government. We all helped each other, worked together and had so much fun together!

Estaban los musicos en los bailes y las fiestas. We had musicians with guitars, violins and accordions at the dances and fiestas. Just about everything was a cause for a feast and celebrating!

Then María Cleofas Sánchez de Aragón's reflections and sentiments steered toward the ageless fandango. The dynamic dance had been performed in New Mexico and all the early colonies of Spain in what was to be called the New World since the first settlement by the Spanish. In New Mexico, this dated to 1598. Fandango dress in Nuevo Mexico was simply the going-out style of the times. Fandango was danced during fiestas. It was danced at weddings. It was danced at religious celebrations and at saints' feast days.

Fandango could take on moods that were solemn, heartbroken and dramatic. In New Mexico, participants used *palmas*, simply clapped their hands and used castanets. Castanets could be any homemade wood instrument that accentuated the sweeping movements.

We all learned how to dance the fandango. Knowing this old dance was a part of our growing up. It took a lot of practice to get it right. Both the boys and girls learned the pasos, the steps that had been passed down in our familias. Once we learned how to do the Fandango, and other dances like La Jota, La Raspa and La Varsoviana, we got ready to go to the dance. My mother sewed our beautiful dresses. My brothers polished their boots with ashes from the stove. We also made opas and ramilletes. These were streamers made with colorful paper with intricate cut out designs.

At the dance, you should have heard the taconazos. Us girls had shoes with big heels so when we danced, the shoes and boots were heard on the wooden floor of the sala, the dance hall that was the living room of the largest house in town, or at the villages' gathering place. Some

Premier flamenco dancer Frances Lujan performs at the Kimo Theater. Frances is distinguished as a trainer, preserver and promoter of folkloric dance and music. *Courtesy Frances Lujan.*

> *homeowners could afford a wood floor so the whole village appreciated him opening his doors for all of us to celebrate. We used palmas to keep up with the beat of the music. We clapped hard. Some had castanets, mantillas, and beautiful fans.*
>
> *¡Estábamos todos tan contentos, apreciábamos todo y siempre le dábamos gracias y gloria a Dios! We were always so happy, we appreciated everything and we always gave glory to God!*

I could picture everything my mother spoke about, especially the joy and happiness created by the festivities of music and dance. The females teased the males when doing the fandango, so my mother laughed while recalling this dance, wherein the girls were coquettes. They flirted through this dance. Intricate pastoral melodies and dance filled with energy, enthusiasm and passion demonstrated the profound influence of Spain that eighteenth-century colonists kept alive in New Mexico. This was continued through their descendants. Males and females challenged one another through the movements of the fandango. In New Mexico, any gathering for dance and celebration became known as a fandango. It is said that this popular Spanish dance incorporated features and movements of the fandango, so there is a clear genealogy still present and visible in New Mexico today. The breathtakingly marvelous horizon of the land paints a picture of fiesta, music and dance.

12

FIESTA EPILOGUE

ormer governor and congressman Bill Richardson spoke glowingly of Edward Lujan of Albuquerque, who has been a strong proponent of preserving the Hispanic culture of New Mexico:

> *Ed Lujan has been involved with the National Hispanic Cultural Center for more than two decades, working for its creation by the state of New Mexico and serving as president of the Center's board since its formation in 1995. Lujan's dream of a thriving Hispanic Cultural Center in Albuquerque's South Valley has become a reality. Ed Lujan and the Cultural Center are synonymous, and I know of no other person who has put more time, effort, and fundraising energy into its development. The National Hispanic Cultural Center has benefited greatly from Lujan's abilities. He was part of a group that secured about $20 million in state funds and $14 million in private funds, including $2.5 million in software and hardware from Intel Corp. Today, the Center, located in Albuquerque along the famed Camino Real, sits on approximately 30 acres of land next to the Rio Grande.*

Now retired, Lujan is the former CEO of Manuel Lujan Agencies, an Albuquerque-based insurance company with offices in Santa Fe, Belen and Taos. The agency, which was purchased by his father in 1926, is a family-run business that started as a one-room operation and has grown into the largest privately owned insurance agency in New Mexico. Stuart Ashman, former New Mexico secretary of the Office of Cultural Affairs, added: "We

The Las Vegas, New Mexico Fourth of July Fiesta features elaborate parade floats. Parade princess Omri de Aragón smiles enthusiastically for the crowds.

are very fortunate to have had an individual like Ed Lujan so committed to moving this Center forward. Along with the rest of the board and the Center's foundation, this institution is poised to make an important mark in the world's understanding and appreciation of the Hispano cultural legacy."

Ralph Arellanes, former state director of the New Mexico chapter of the League of United Latin American Citizens (LULAC), the oldest national Hispanic organization for civil rights, recently wrote:

I fondly remember the Fourth of July Fiestas de Las Vegas, New Mexico in such a beautiful way. I grew up two blocks south of the Old Town Plaza so we could hear every Hispano band playing and see the entertainment and performers from the morning until midnight. I grew up in a huge family of six brothers, one sister and my parents, José Espiridion Arellanes, and Stella Clara Gallegos Arellanes, so it was great we could walk to the fiestas any time of the day. We would see friends, young and old and from near and far at the plaza park. The parades for fiestas were awesome. And they included many high school bands and majorettes from Mora, Pecos, Wagon Mound, Ratón, Santa Fe, and other nearby towns and cities. The New Mexico Highlands University marching band was always a highlight. The constant smell of hamburgers and cotton candy added to the excitement. The Fiestas de Las Vegas are from days of the most authentic celebrations of our history, heritage, and culture. With the last night of fiestas with fireworks over the nearby beautiful and scenic Storrie Lake, my childhood dream is always replayed each and every year.

Ralph Arrellanes has had a distinguished career and is actively involved in New Mexico as a prominent civic leader and supporter of Latino civil rights in the country. He was elected state director of IMAGE, the incorporated National Mexican American Employees organization. He is currently chairman of the Hispanic Roundtable of New Mexico, a coalition of local, state and national Hispanic organizations. Edward I. Romero, former U.S. ambassador to Spain, said of Arellano, "He has been a very strong leader in safeguarding Hispanic heritage in New Mexico." Ralph's father, Espiridion, and his uncle George Arellanes both served in World War II, and his mother, Stella Clara, was a riveter at Rocky Mountain Arsenal at Rocky Flats, Colorado. They were honored at the Fourth of July Fiestas in Las Vegas, New Mexico.

When one goes to the fiestas in Old Town Albuquerque and other events, one cannot escape the broad smile and welcoming arms of Jesús "Chuy" Martínez. No one would even realize that this soft-spoken individual has not only won many awards but also is a recognized fixture in Albuquerque and New Mexico arts. He is a popular singer, songwriter and folklorist. Chuy, as everyone calls him, served as associate curator of education at the Albuquerque Museum. He was the events supervisor for the Albuquerque Cultural Services Department. He has hosted the television series *Caminos Culturales* and has produced and hosted the popular TV show *Lo Maduro de la Cultura*, which features the best of culture. Chuy has been the recipient of the Lifetime Achievement Award given by Hilos Culturales, the Human Rights Unsung Hero Award, the Bravo Artist of the Year award, the Community Service Award, the Ohti Award and several others. Despite his numerous awards, Chuy is most at ease and happy seeing others, especially families and children, enjoying themselves and having a good time at fiestas.

Chuy Martínez has had a long and distinguished career. Besides producing several recordings, he was an activist during the civil rights movement of the 1960s. In California, Chuy joined Cesar Chávez, played his guitar and sang at United Farmworkers gatherings. In New Mexico, the well-known singer acted with La Companía de Teatro de Alburquerque, the highly acclaimed grassroots theater group stimulated by Dr. Miguel Encinias and actor José

Right: Chuy Martínez is past producer and host of the TV show *Lo Maduro de la Cultura*. He now hosts and produces *Caminos Culturales* and performs at festivals. *Courtesy of Chuy Martínez*.

Below: Xiomara Fortuna, "Queen of Fusion," accompanied by Claudio Toulouse on guitar, Arnaldo Acosta on drums and Magic Mejia, at the 2022 AfroMundo Festival in Albuquerque. AfroMundo celebrates Black/Latino culture in New Mexico. *Courtesy Loida Maritza Pérez*.

Rodríguez, who was trained at the Royal Academy in London. La Companía exposed students, children and adults to the theater throughout New Mexico and nearby states. Chuy has much to be proud of, but what gives him the greatest pride is in helping to stimulate the arts for others in the state through additional opportunities for festivities and celebrations. Chuy has partnered with highly acclaimed Loida Maritza Pérez in this regard.

Maritza is the founder and executive director of AfroMundo, an active organization interested in fostering civic engagement and diverse cultures. She is the author of *Geographies of Home*, which was featured in the *New York Times*. A forthcoming book is *Beyond the Pale*, which won a PEN America 2019 Jean Stein Grant for Literary Oral History. She is the recipient of numerous awards and fellowships, including from the National Endowment for the Arts in collaboration with the University of New Mexico and Rutgers University. Loida Maritza Pérez attended Cornell University, was published in *Latina Magazine* and *The Oxford Encyclopedia of Latinos and Latinas in the United States*. She edited *Reflections on Water*, an anthology of poetry, prose and art promoting conservation and awareness of water issues in New Mexico. For the inaugural AfroMundo 2022 Festival, several events, including music, dance, film, culinary feasts and world-class performers, were featured in Albuquerque.

World-class performer Xiomara Fortuna, "La Reina de la Fusión" (The Queen of Fusion) was a headliner during the AfroMundo 2022 Festival. The organization promotes a multigenerational collective of tradition bearers, storytellers, community historians, artists, cultural specialists and humanities scholars. Afro-Dominican singer and composer Xiomara Fortuna participated as a speaker at the Latin American and Iberian Institute at the University of New Mexico. Her first exposure was to Dominican folk music. From Dominican rhythms, she went into experimenting with Caribbean music, including Jamaican songs and melodies. Her music is called Música Raíz (musical roots) and incorporates merengue, son, samba, reggae and contemporary fusion music. Loida Maritza Pérez and others are determined to expose the New Mexico public to recording artists and professionals recognized internationally and featured in Albuquerque and New Mexico fiestas and events, thereby raising already popular events to a higher level. Another person blazing trails is Afro Latina artist, teacher and chorographer Yvonne Gutiérrez. She is a member of NAEYC (International Association of Blacks in Dance Inc.). She is also with the Black Flamenco Network, served as a panelist for the thirty-fourth annual Festival Flamenco in Albuquerque and was with the New Perspectives in

Above: Singer-performer Wil Tabares sings songs at events from his award-winning CD *La Luz de la Luna*. Wil performed in the musicals *Evita*, *Grease* and *Jesus Christ Superstar*. *Courtesy of Wil Tabares.*

Left: Dance Magazine selected Yvonne Gutiérrez as an award honoree. A founding member of the Black Flamenco Network, she was accompanied by Tito Puente. *Photo by ItzILa Gutierrez. Courtesy of Yvonne Gutiérrez.*

Flamenco History and Research Symposium. She is a faculty member at the Ballet Hispanic School of Dance and is associated with FUAAD (Flamencos Unidos Africanos y Afro Descendientes) (United African Flamencos, and Afro Descendants). Yvonne Gutiérrez combines elements of ballet, flamenco, castanets and shawls. She won the *Dance Magazine* 2022 Dance Teacher Award. She is a heralded flamenco, salsa and Spanish dance artist distinguished for serving overlooked communities. AfroMundo's theme for 2023 is "Resistance and Creativity."

Flamenco swept into New Mexico many decades ago and experienced enormous popularity. Dancers such as José Greco, María Benítez, Lilli del Castillo and others have graced and performed on main stages in Santa Fe, Albuquerque, nationally and internationally. Some flamenco performers have come directly from Spain, but others have been New Mexico natives, such as Isabel Lujan. She traveled to Spain, trained there and then went on tour. She met José "El Pelete" Arencón. José Arencón was born in Almendralejo, Bajados, Spain. He distinguished himself by learning and breathing flamenco dance, singing flamenco and playing flamenco guitar. He wowed audiences by doing all three on stage at the same time. El Pelete and Isabel Lujan were married in Madrid in 1974. They moved to Albuquerque, where Isabel opened a flamenco school. One of her distinguished students was Albuquerque native Wil Tabares. Through the years, many other flamenco schools and academies have opened in New Mexico. A native student who is a prime performer at the Tablao Flamenco held regularly at Hotel Albuquerque is guitarist Estevan Pacheco. He is accompanied by other dancers and singers. Flamenco schools in Albuquerque are dedicated to empowering and inspiring native success. Pacheco performed at DCINY (Distinguished Concert International in New York City). He was a valedictorian at the Tierra Adentro School, which has a distinguished flamenco curriculum from grade school through high school. The University of New Mexico senior teaches flamenco guitar to others and performs throughout the state at festivals, fairs and fiestas.

The premier Latina playwright, producer and director of New Mexico Hispanic stage productions is Rosa María Calles. The Tomé, New Mexico native has been featured in numerous publications and has been praised by many critics. Her long-running and successful stage production *Cuento de la Llorona* (*Tale of the Wailing Woman*) continually experienced sold-out shows at the Ilfeld Auditorium in Las Vegas, the Lensic in Santa Fe, the Kimo in Albuquerque and many other venues, including the National Hispanic Culture Center. Calles caught the eye of the media in many ways.

From left to right: guitarist Estevan Pacheco, Rocki Jian, Cory McBride and Ysabela Trujillo. Estevan has gained rapid fame. He performed at Distinguished Concert International at Carnegie Hall.

The widely acclaimed playwright sought grassroots actors with no stage experience. Calles said she wanted nurses, teachers, bus drivers and mechanics—people from all walks of life who always dreamed of performing in front of an audience. Those in the know said Rosa María Calles was doomed to failure. They also warned that she would not be able to produce a massive undertaking without funding. She proved everyone wrong. "I am a workaholic, and when I make up my mind on doing something I'll even sew the costumes and do whatever it takes." Rosa was stunned by the positive response she received from the public. Everyone jumped on the bandwagon.

Her fantastic drama took a popular Latino ghost story and transformed it for the stage. This meant dialogue in both English and Spanish, and she wanted not only the folklore but also song, music and dance. Rosa was inundated with those wanting to perform. She made it work, with over fifty performers, including stage crew. Calles did not turn anyone away. Even children, youth, the elderly and families were actively involved in all facets, including advertising and promotion. *Cuento de La Llorona* was so successful that Calles was invited to perform her show at the Ricardo Montalbán

Rosalía de Aragón, sponsored by the New Mexico Humanities Council and promoted by the Center of Latino Initiatives, performed at the Smithsonian in 2003.

Theater in Hollywood. The popular event was sponsored by Walt Disney Studios, and the play was promoted by the Spanish television networks *Univisión* and *Televisión*.

In Albuquerque and throughout New Mexico, Rosa María Calles often held the performance in conjunction with other fiestas or events, such as the International Balloon Fiesta. "We had to provide some other place for balloonists and others to go to for other fun and entertainment," Calles said. She was featured in *Cultural Insights: Latinos in the Industry* in Los Angeles; *Guest Life*, a publication placed in all New Mexico hotels and motels; a travel guide for tourists published in New York; and in a special feature in *New Mexico Magazine* on the most famous ghost tale of the state and in the Spanish-speaking world.

It is no wonder why New Mexico, with its climate, environment, wondrous Native American cultures and fantastic Spanish history, has attracted so many. Black history is personified with the founding of the city of Blackdom, where Black Americans sought a future for themselves and their children.

Folk band Bayou Seco performs with iconic Antonia Apodaca on accordion. Bayou Seco has received many awards playing at folk music festivals and celebrations. Antonia was proclaimed a "Living Legend" by the State of New Mexico. *Courtesy of Bayou Seco.*

New Mexico has attracted people not only from other states but also from around the world. Ken Keppler and Jeanie McLerie, who were already established and successful musicians in the South, made a trip to New Mexico. "We fell in love with the place," Jeanie said. They settled in Silver City and profoundly contributed to the fabric and culture of the state. Ken and Jeanie traveled throughout the state to isolated mountain towns and picturesque villages. They introduced themselves and, like all musicians and singers, were graciously accepted with smiles and open arms. The extremely sociable couple introduced cajón music and other forms such as jazz to local musicians and singers, who had always been open to everything in music and song, as were their ancestors. Ken and Jeanie also built up their marvelous repertoire. Then, Bayou Seco was founded and created.

Bayou Seco, a group of professional musicians and singers led by Ken and Jeanie, travels throughout New Mexico, entertaining at trade fairs, folk festivals, farmers markets and anywhere and everywhere. The band describes its format: "Fiddling friends, joyous compadres, and simply showing respect for all cross-cultural music. For nearly forty years we have played Cajun two-steps, waltzes, polkas, rancheras, chotis, merengue, huapangos, the old Broom Dance, and the Vals de los Paños, The Handkerchief Waltz. We have invited one and all to sing, play with us, and dance. We all have such a good time, and so much fun!" As ambassadors of New Mexico music, Bayou Seco received the Governor's Award for Excellence in the Arts. "We want to preserve Hispanic and Cowboy folk music plus the Spanish Colonial dance and songs of New Mexico for generations to come!" Jeanie very proudly expounds, "This is what New Mexico Fiesta is all about!"

13

NEW MEXICO GUIDE TO FIESTAS

Fiestas and celebrations at Hispanic and Indian villages, towns and cities are dedicated to certain events. Festivities that take place in many areas throughout the year may revolve around Catholic feast days. Many communities, including Indian pueblos, are named after saints, for example, Nuestra Señora de los Dolores de Las Vegas (Our Lady of Sorrows of the Meadows). The city is now simply known as Las Vegas. Each year, this city in northern New Mexico celebrates the Our Lady of Sorrows Fiesta with food, music, dance and games. This event has taken place since about 1840, soon after the town was founded in 1835.

The Fiesta de Tomé and the San Felipe Fiesta in Old Town Albuquerque are probably the oldest New Mexico fiestas other than the Fiesta de Santa Fe and date variously back to the late eighteenth century. Most Hispanic village fiestas date to the nineteenth century. Indian villages, because of the Spanish mission churches dating to the seventeenth and eighteenth centuries, have older ritual festivals on saints' days. Native American tribes, of course, have festivities and celebrations dating back hundreds and even thousands of years in New Mexico. A very appropriate statement that coincides with both Spanish fiestas and Indian rituals was made by highly acclaimed Native American researcher and historian Joe Sando: "The knowledge of a spiritual life is part of the person twenty-four hours a day, every day of the year. In describing the beliefs and practices of today the traditional religion may also be understood. There is little basic change. The tradition of religious belief permeates every aspect of the people's life; it determines man's relation with the natural world and with fellow man. Its basic concern is continuity of a

«Alli viene la mujer...»

La Llorona Festival

October 12, 2002

The Las Vegas Festival celebrates La Llorona, the Wailing Woman, a legendary ghost. Emilio Aragón, Harvest Festival of Las Vegas organizer, and others keep heritage and culture alive. *Courtesy of Rosalía de Aragón.*

harmonious relationship with the world in which man lives."

When Dr. Joe Sando spoke with me many years ago, he talked about Spanish and Pueblo Indian history. He genuinely believed that both histories had separate and marvelous identities. During the four-hundred-plus-year history of the Spanish and the Indians, Dr. Sando firmly believed, both cultures complemented each other and other cultures for the greater common good.

Dr. Sando was always for equal justice, human rights and peace and harmony. Many called him a civil rights leader, but he said, "I am simply an Indian." He called to confirm spirit holidays such as fiestas and times for everyone to sing and dance, to be joyous and to always be in harmony with the earth. The following is certainly not meant to be a complete list but serves to provide a sampling of annual fiestas, festivals and celebrations in the Land of Enchantment.

ENERO (JANUARY)
Padre Don Antonio José Martínez Day, commemorating the birth of New Mexico's folk hero priest in 1793
Taos Pueblo, Turtle Dance, January 1
Santo Domingo Pueblo, Corn Dance, January 1
San Juan Pueblo, Cloud & Basket Dance, January 1
Picuris Pueblo Rituals, January 6
Nambe Pueblo, Antelope, Buffalo and Deer Dances, January 6
Sandia Pueblo Rituals, January 6
Taos Pueblo, Buffalo and Deer Dances, January 6
San Ildefonso Pueblo, Saint's Feast Day, January 23

FEBRERO (FEBRUARY)
San Felipe and Picuris Pueblos, Día de Candelaria Celebration, Candlemas, February 2. This Catholic festival commemorates the presentation of the Christ child at the Temple.

In 1990, the Las Vegas, New Mexico Fiesta council selected Rosa María Calles as the poster artist. Twenty-five thousand prints of *Fiesta, Música y Baile* were sold.

Marzo (March)
Laguna Pueblo, Harvest Dance, March 19
Village of San José Feast Day, March 19

Abril (April)
Village of San Juan Feast Day, April 7
Afro Mundo Festival, April 15–22

Mayo (May)
San Felipe Pueblo, Día de San Felipe (Saint Philip's Day), May 1
Taos Pueblo, Blessing of the Fields, Santa Cruz, Holy Cross Feast Day, May 3
Cinco de Mayo, events statewide, May 5
Córdova, Fiesta de San Ysidro, May 13
San Isidro, May 15

Junio (June)
Sandia Pueblo, San Antonio, Saint Anthony's Feast Day, June 13
Santa Clara Pueblo Ritual Dances, June 13
Picuris Pueblo, Foot Races, June 13
Fiestas de San Juan, various towns, June 24
San Juan Pueblo, Saint John Feast Day, Corn Dances, June 24
Santa Ana Pueblo, Saint Anne's Feast Day, June 29

Julio (July)
Nambe Pueblo, Celebration of the Waterfall, changing date
Mescalero Apache, Mountain Spirits, July 4
Las Vegas, Fourth of July Fiestas, July 4
Mescalero Apache Maiden Rites and Mountain Spirit Dance, July 4
Picuris Pueblo Village Arts, July 4
Taos Pueblo Intertribal Pow Wow, July 9–11
Cochiti Pueblo, San Buenaventura, Saint Bonaventure Feast Day, July 14
Jicarilla Apache Ritual Dances and Roundup, July 15–18
San Juan Pueblo, Northern Indian Pueblos Fair, July 17–18
Santiago, Saint James Feast Day, Taos and other pueblos, July 25
Santa Ana and Laguna Pueblo, Saint Ann Feast Day, July 26

Agosto (August)
Fiestas de Santa Fe, August 4 to 8

Lucia de Aragón, born in 1898 in Las Vegas, New Mexico, learned traditional folk dancing and then danced on stages in New York City and in other countries.

Pat Reyes with Luna Upfront performs at the St. Therese Parish Fiesta in Albuquerque. Church saint feast days are widely popular, including at Indian pueblos. *Courtesy of Reverend Vincent Paul Chávez.*

SEPTIEMBRE (SEPTEMBER)
Tomé, Feast of the Nativity of the Blessed Virgin, September 8
Cañones, Fiesta de San Miguel, September 29
Taos San Geronimo, September 30

OCTUBRE (OCTOBER)
Albuquerque International Balloon Fiestas, October
St. Therese of the Infant Jesus Church Feast Day, October 1
Nambe Pueblo, Feast of San Francisco, October 4
Álamo Navajo Indian Day, October 10–11
Dia de la Raza, Columbus Day, October 12

NOVIEMBRE (NOVEMBER)
Tesuque Pueblo, San Diego Feast Day, November 13
Zuni Pueblo, Luminarias & Lights, November 27

DICIEMBRE (DECEMBER)
Pojoaque Pueblo, Annual Saints' Feast Day, December 11
Nuestra Señora de Guadalupe Feast Day, events statewide, December 12
Las Posadas, events statewide, December 16–24
Luminaria Light Parades, events statewide, December 24

SELECTED REFERENCES

Cabeza de Baca, Fabiola. *The Good Life and Food*. Santa Fe: Museum of New Mexico Press, 2005.

———. *Historic Cookery*. Las Vegas, NM: Los Artesanos, 1970.

———. *We Fed Them Cactus*. Albuquerque: University of New Mexico Press, 1998.

Chavez, Fray Angelico. *Origins of New Mexico Families in the Spanish Colonial Period*. Santa Fe: Historical Society of New Mexico, 1954.

de Baca, Vincent C. *La Gente Hispano History and Life in Colorado*. Denver: Colorado Historical Society, 1988.

Edwards, Gwynne, and Ken Haas. *Flamenco!*. New York: Thames & Hudson, 2000.

Ferguson, Erna. *New Mexico: A Pageant of Three Peoples*. Albuquerque: University of New Mexico Press, 1973.

Foor, Francis. *A Treasury of Mexican Folkways*. New York: Crown, 1947.

Gonzales, Samuel Leo. *The Days of Old*. Trementina, NM: privately printed, 1993.

Grut, Marina. *The Bolero School*. London: Dance Books, 2002.

Hazen-Hammond. *A Short History of Santa Fe*. San Francisco, CA: Lexicos, 1988.

Jaramillo Hughes, Linda. *Recetas y Recuerdos, Recipes, and Memories*. Belen, NM: self-published, n.d.

Kutsche, Paul, and John R. Van Ness. *Canones—Values, Crisis, and Survival in a Northern New Mexico Village*. Albuquerque: University of New Mexico Press, 1981.

La Farge, Oliver. *Santa Fe: The Autobiography of a Southwestern Town*. Norman: University of Oklahoma Press, 1959.

Lucero, Aurora. *Los Hispanos*. Denver, CO: Sage Books, 1947.

Menard, Valerie. Foreword by Cheech Marin. *The Latino Holiday Book*. New York: Marlowe & Company, 2000.

Milne, Jean. *Fiesta Time in Latin America*. Los Angeles: Ward Ritchie Press, 1965.

Nostrand, Richard L. *The Hispano Homeland*. Norman: University of Oklahoma Press, 1992.

Nusom, Lynn. *Christmas in New Mexico*. Phoenix, AZ: Golden West Publishers, 1991.

Ribera Ortega, Pedro. *Christmas in Old Santa Fe*. Santa Fe, NM: Sunstone Press, 1973.

Romero, Philomena. *New Mexican Dishes*. Los Alamos, NM: self-published, 1970.

Simmons, Marc, and Frank Turley. *Southwestern Colonial Ironwork*. Santa Fe: Museum of New Mexico, 1980.

Stapleton, Ernest, and John Mondragon. *Public Education in New Mexico*. Albuquerque: University of New Mexico Press, 2005.

Warren, Nancy Hunter. *Villages of Hispanic New Mexico*. Santa Fe, NM: School of American Research Press, 1987.

Weigle, Marta, and Peter White. *The Lore of New Mexico*. Albuquerque: University of New Mexico Press, 2003.

ABOUT THE AUTHOR

ay John de Aragón served as the activities director at the University of Albuquerque. This was an elected position through the student senate. He was also a talent scout and coach for the Upward Bound program at the university. He served as president of the New Mexico Spanish Colonial Arts Guild, an organization dedicated to the preservation of the traditional Hispanic folk culture, music and dance. He was also president of Matraka Inc., a nonprofit serving the community in the preservation of the arts. Ray John was actively involved with the New Mexico Arts Division and was appointed to serve on the New Mexico Arts Council and the New Mexico Arts Alliance by former governor Susana Martinez. Ray John de Aragón founded the Southwest Hispanic Culture Festival, which was held at the Armand Hammer United World College of the American West. He was the literary chairman of the Feria Artesana, the largest Hispanic arts festival in the country, held at the Albuquerque Convention Center and sponsored by the City of Albuquerque.

Visit us at
www.historypress.com